MARY

The Chosen Woman

The Mother of Jesus in the Quran

وَإِذْ قَالَتِ
ٱلْمَلَٰٓئِكَةُ يَٰمَرْيَمُ إِنَّ ٱللَّهَ ٱصْطَفَىٰكِ وَطَهَّرَكِ وَٱصْطَفَىٰكِ
عَلَىٰ نِسَآءِ ٱلْعَٰلَمِينَ ﴿٤٢﴾ يَٰمَرْيَمُ ٱقْنُتِى لِرَبِّكِ وَٱسْجُدِى
وَٱرْكَعِى مَعَ ٱلرَّٰكِعِينَ ﴿٤٣﴾ ذَٰلِكَ مِنْ أَنۢبَآءِ ٱلْغَيْبِ نُوحِيهِ
إِلَيْكَ ۚ وَمَا كُنتَ لَدَيْهِمْ إِذْ يُلْقُونَ أَقْلَٰمَهُمْ أَيُّهُمْ يَكْفُلُ
مَرْيَمَ ۖ وَمَا كُنتَ لَدَيْهِمْ إِذْ يَخْتَصِمُونَ ﴿٤٤﴾ إِذْ قَالَتِ
ٱلْمَلَٰٓئِكَةُ يَٰمَرْيَمُ إِنَّ ٱللَّهَ يُبَشِّرُكِ بِكَلِمَةٍ مِّنْهُ ٱسْمُهُ ٱلْمَسِيحُ
عِيسَى ٱبْنُ مَرْيَمَ وَجِيهًا فِى ٱلدُّنْيَا وَٱلْءَاخِرَةِ وَمِنَ ٱلْمُقَرَّبِينَ ﴿٤٥﴾
وَيُكَلِّمُ ٱلنَّاسَ فِى ٱلْمَهْدِ وَكَهْلًا وَمِنَ ٱلصَّٰلِحِينَ ﴿٤٦﴾

And behold, the angels said, "O Mary, indeed God has chosen you and purified you and has chosen you above the women of the world. O Mary, have reverence for your Lord and bow down ˹to Him˺; and bow with those who bow." This is of the tidings of the unseen We reveal to you, ˹O Muḥammad˺. And you were not with them when they were casting their quills ˹to determine˺ which of them would have the care of Mary. And you were not with them when they were contending. Behold, the angels said, "O Mary, indeed God gives you glad tidings of a word from Him; his name is the Messiah, son of Mary, eminent in this world and the Hereafter and he is of those drawn near. And he shall speak to people in the cradle and as a grown man, and he shall be of the righteous."

(Quran, 3:42–46)

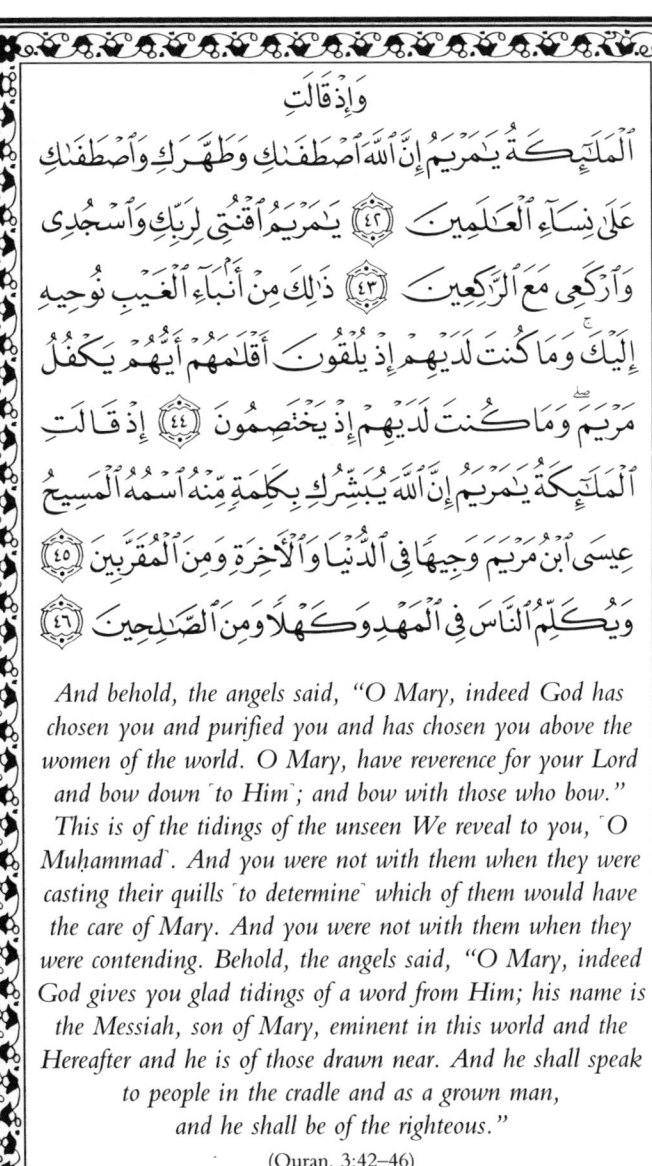

MARY

The Chosen Woman

The Mother of Jesus in the Quran

An Interlinear Commentary on Sûrat Maryam

Ahmad Zaki Hammad

Printed in the United States of America

Published by: Quranic Literacy Institute (QLI)
P.O. Box 1467
Bridgeview, Illinois 60455 • U.S.A.
(708) 430-1991 • (708) 430-1992 (Fax)

Book Editors: Amer A. Haleem & Ibrahim N. Abusharif

ISBN (soft cover): 0-9650746-8-4

The text is set in Bembospecial, a type that facilitates Arabic transliteration and the use of features special to Islamic literature, such as " ﷺ " and " عليه السلام ".

FOR

*All in the English-speaking world—
especially young people—who may find in
this story the resolve to seek divine
guidance for a meaningful life,
here and in the Hereafter.*

AND FOR

*Professor Muhammad Qutb, who at age 80 is
still young at heart, and who with his endless
love for the Quran, his penetrating insight
into it, and his reflection of the Quran's spirit
of moderation and morality
is a source of inspiration.*

AND FOR

*Asmâ', my grandchild, who has so recently
been added into these youthful ranks,
bringing light and joy into our lives. Seek in
Maryam your example of loving worship,
moral purity, and undaunted striving for
nearness to God, and you shall be
forever blessed.*

TRANSLITERATION NOTE

The transliteration of Arabic names and terms into English follows a well-established scheme shown below. Also, nearly every mention of the name of Prophet Muḥammad ﷺ is followed by the Arabic " ﷺ " which may be translated as "God bless him and give him peace," a prayer of endearment reflecting Muslim veneration for the Prophet ﷺ. Likewise, out of veneration " ﵇ " may appear after the names of other prophets mentioned (as well as Angel Gabriel ﵇), and it basically means "peace be upon him."

ء	’	ض	ḍ
ا	â *or* a	ط	ṭ
ب	b	ظ	ẓ
ت	t	ع	ʿ
ث	th	غ	gh
ج	j	ف	f
ح	ḥ	ق	q
خ	kh	ك	k
د	d	ل	l
ذ	dh	م	m
ر	r	ن	n
ز	z	ه	h
س	s	و	û *or* u w *(consonant)*
ش	sh	ى	î *or* i *or* iyy y *(consonant)*
ص	ṣ		

QURANIC CITATION NOTE

References to the Quran's verses in this book are cited following an established numerical system. For example, the *third verse* of the Quran's *first sura* (or chapter) is cited as *Quran, 1:3* (the sura number followed by the number of the verse, separated by a colon).

BRACKETS NOTE

Within several translated texts are half brackets ⌜ ⌝ that contain clarifying text that should be read as if it were part of the text. For example: *It is He who sends prayers ⌜of blessings⌝ down upon you*…(Quran, 33:43).

CONTENTS

PREFACE .... *ix*

Sûrat Maryam, the nineteenth chapter of the Quran, introduces a wondrous understanding of the physical world that cannot be known except by divine revelation. It is centered on the fact that the objects of creation—such as the mountains and the sky—have *self-awareness*. They are worshippers of God aware of their purpose and the oneness of their Maker. Such a marvelous revelation of our surrounding expands (or so it should) our thought life and our sciences. This is a view that engenders an optimism that is simply impossible with ideologies that propose a universe as an accidental outcome.

INTRODUCTION *1*

Mary and Jesus: A mother and her son. For much of the world and for many long centuries, a divisive and often acrimonious dispute has centered on these two great human beings. To sincerely embrace and ponder the truth about Mary, as preserved in the Quran, is an exercise in spiritual development. Mary's honor, morality, patience, resolve, gentleness, and love make her a model for the seeker of any age, geography, or gender.

OVERVIEW *15*

The chapter of Mary in the Quran holds a special place in the hearts and history of Muslims. A passage of 98 verses, the sura establishes for a final and sweeping time what all the prophets (including Jesus ﷺ) have taught, that God is God and everything else is not. The themes of Sûrat Maryam are here expanded upon, as is the context of its revelation from God to the Prophet Muḥammad ﷺ.

INTERLINEAR COMMENTARY

A close translation of the meaning of the sura with explanatory interjections and elaborations of key concepts based on authoritative commentaries and sound scholarship. The commentary is divided into the following sections.

INTERPRETATION

The translation of the meaning of the sura standing alone without the additional explanations.

APPENDIX

A concise analysis of the biblical account of the genealogy of Mary, in comparison with the Quranic narration.

BIBLIOGRAPHY

INDEX

PREFACE

The Miracle of Creation

The human creation is a being of limitations that God has endued with creative consciousness. This union of constraint and ranging imagination makes discovery an interesting part of our very essence. The instruments, techniques, and culture of curiosity we have devised to satisfy this exploration instinct have vastly expanded our awareness of the secrets of the physical world. Unseen structures of matter are continually discerned at previously impregnable levels; forces, energies, and dimensions that shape material existence are continually theorized, tested, and recast; human understanding of the invisible mechanisms and connections that bring the universe into seamless coherence are hypothesized, debunked, and postulated again—such that steadily, inevitably existence yields her enigmatic attributes to our mortal minds.

The scientific sensibility, for the most part, has evolved enough (at least for peer review purposes, if for no higher reason) to restrain researchers who would otherwise rush fecklessly to state the "last word" on the natural world. There are, however, scientists who have grown too wise to deny transcendent meaning and purpose in existence, and who have realized that to allege the opposite, based entirely upon lab- or fieldwork, is to overreach the competence of empirical inquiry.[1] One of modern science's most lauded breakthroughs in these early days of the new millennium, for example, has been the declared completion of the project to map out the human genetic code, or genome. This has enabled us for the first time to decipher in a rather comprehensive manner the relationship connecting sequences of vital molecules in our cells to our physical attributes and conditions. Interestingly, one of the project's directors heralded this achievement with the words, "Today we celebrate the first glimpse of our instruction book, previously known only to God."[2] If one listens past the seeming arrogance of these words for a moment, one hears a new tone that has slowly emerged among the scientists of our time; namely, a humbling recognition that the mere proportion of what is unknown about creation far outstrips all human comprehension of it. However reluctant or incidental this concession may be, it pointedly underscores the need for religion (and philosophy within the realm of its competency) to recover the right to contemplate the findings of science and relate them to truths known to man only by way of revelation and informed reflection.

Indeed, human discovery of the natural world deepens the religious experience because it heightens our realization of the existence of system, complexity, harmony, order, and magnitude in creation on a scale that seriously dents (if not outright dismisses) the theories of an accidental universe. Natural inquiry, unfettered by anthropological agendas, has the capacity to inform and affirm the recognition of divine purpose in creation—a recognition found in all human beings. Such an optimistic, congruous, and innate view of existence is perhaps the antidote to a terrible sense of alienation and the myriad personal psychoses and social turmoil that have resulted from this disaffection. What truth or hope can possibly inhabit a view of ourselves as fleeting organic luck adrift in endless space? The God-given impulse to understand our surroundings serves to relocate our spiritual selves and earthly purpose in a colossal universe. This impulse to "know," when guided by revelation, shall conduct us to the eventuality we so crave—coming near to our sole and resplendent Maker.

Revelation and Knowledge

Revelation is a term that has been clouded over in the modern lexicon because it essentially has been removed from modernity's ledger of accepted sources of knowledge. In a word, revealed knowledge is to be understood as that divine inspiration that God imparted to humankind through His prophets and messengers and the revealed Books they left behind. Though these streams have ceased to flow anew from God to humanity, their final expressions have been preserved in the 114 chapters of the scripture known as *the Quran* and in the authentic statements and deeds of the Prophet Muḥammad ﷺ. The latter expression is known as the *Sunna*. Part of this enduring act of mercy to humankind is that God has revealed so much about creation in the Quran—both what can be known by way of observation and what is known only by way of divine revelation.

From this revealed knowledge, there is the impeccable and optimistic report from the unseen that every constituent of the universe has a vital and active awareness of its special purpose in existence and of its veneration and servitude to God, the Creator. If the enchantment of the universe comes as a surprise to the human being, this wonderment derives from a careless projection of his own centric sense of consciousness onto other creatures, and from constructing a *comprehensive* understanding of them by what little is really known. The human being is prone to be remiss about some realities, among these is that the self-awareness of each member of creation befits its own nature and need not resemble the consciousness or existence peculiar to humans.

All the diverse kinds and ways of cognizance within creation, however, come to a common point, the Quran tells us; namely, the recognition that all creation has the self-same Creator, who is one and without peer. Thus, at the moment a person bears witness that God is one, this human creature swings into harmony with the entirety of creation. For God is the one who has brought all things into existence and shaped them and their destinies.

It is to this reality that Moses testifies when he tells Pharaoh, *"Our Lord is He who gave everything its creation, then guided it"* (Quran, 20:53). And the Quran instructs the Prophet Muḥammad ﷺ to *glorify the name of your Lord the Most High, who created then gave form, and who determined then guided* (Quran, 87:1–3). Moreover, the Quran informs us that some creatures, like human beings, possess volition in addition to consciousness, that is, the power to intend to do or not to do, while others carry out their assigned purposes unfailingly, never given a choice, like the angels. For example, the heavens, the earth, the mountains, and rivers; the oceans, clouds, and all the elements of chemistry—each fulfills its function and obeys its properties for the duration of its existence (miracles notwithstanding).

Thus the Quran divulges to us mysteries of the universe that empirical methods are incapable of conveying. It is only with revealed knowledge that our interior senses are primed to perceive guidance. The Quran teaches us, for instance, that before the creation of human beings, God offered the "trust" of choice and free will to the heavens, the earth, and the mountains. But they refused, perhaps because they were judicious about the enormity of such a trust and its weighty consequence. So they preferred to remain in existence as they are: Conscious heavens, conscious earth, conscious mountains; conscious of their being, their destiny, and their common Creator—conscious, yet powerless to do other than what God has created them to do and what He commands them: *Indeed, We offered the trust ˹of volitional faith˺ to the heavens and the earth and the mountains, but they refused to bear it and were fearful of it* (Quran, 33:72). Theirs is but to extol the majesty of their Lord and worship Him without ever transgressing, spreading corruption, or committing sin: *Do you not see that whoever is in the heavens and the earth glorify God, and ˹so too˺ the birds outspreading ˹their wings˺! Each one of them has known its ˹way of˺ prayer and glorification. And God is all-knowing of what they do* (Quran, 24:41). *And to Him belongs whoever is in the heavens and the earth. All are reverential to Him* (Quran, 30:26).

This sky above us, this earth beneath our feet, these mountains towering overhead—what they declined, we human beings hastily accepted. We have made a solemn covenant with God before our physical existence on earth; the agreement is imprinted upon our souls that we volitional men and women are to believe in God as He is—one, all-forgiving, all-merciful, and all-powerful—and are *not* to commit idolatry, invent divine attributes, assign partners to God, or worship anything apart from Him. Hence, creation itself loathes it when human beings make false attributions with God—be it the claim of a son, a mother, a consort, an idol, or His nonexistence—when in no way does this befit the Lord of the Worlds. This is the reality that antecedes the reaction of creation, the nearly cataclysmic recoiling of the heavens, earth, and mountains from the appalling attributions that human beings recklessly ascribe to God, assaulting His majesty. We are not yet equipped to read nature's reaction, so the Quran transcribes it for us with heart-quavering imagery in a spectacular passage of Sûrat Maryam, the chapter of the Quran named after Mary, the mother of Jesus, which is the subject of this book:

> *And they have said, "The All-Merciful has taken a son." Truly you have come with something abominable. From it the heavens nearly burst, and the earth ˹nearly˺ splits and the mountains ˹all but˺ fall down, collapsing—that ˹people˺ should ascribe to the All-Merciful a son, while it is not befitting to the All-Merciful that He take a son. Indeed, each one in the heavens and the earth but comes to the All-Merciful as a servant. Truly, He has enumerated them, and He has numbered them with a precise number. And each one of them is coming to Him on the Day of Resurrection alone.* (Quran, 19:88–96)

Here dwells the overarching aim of Sûrat Maryam: To remind humanity—especially those who would truly follow the son of Mary—that the most essential truth of which the entirety of existence is conscious is that its Creator is one, indivisible, and eternally so. God's relationship to His creation does not consist of Him begetting or incarnating into created forms and phases of development. On the contrary, God is utterly without rival or associate of any sort. None shares with Him in His divinity. There is but one relationship between God and all other existence, namely, that of Creator and created; and none but He can enumerate all the constituents of existence, which are forever dependent upon Him. For everything in creation is hurtling toward God. The meeting point is the ultimate destiny of the Hereafter, a day in which all debates shall be settled and all deeds requited.

God, the Sole Creator, is all-merciful and mercy-giving. He has sent human guides descended from Adam, the first man. These are the elect believers who place their faith in none but God and live righteous lives, employing themselves toward good works. God chose them that they may lead their peoples out of the veils of darkness and into the light of the straight way. Sûrat Maryam hallows the names of some of these chosen ones, who are humanity's true forebears: Noah, Idrîs (Enoch?), Abraham, Ishmael, Isaac, Jacob, Moses, Aaron, Zachariah, John, Mary, and Jesus, peace be upon them all:

> *These are the ones upon whom God bestowed grace—from the prophets of the children of Adam, and from those whom We carried with Noah, and from the children of Abraham and Israel, and from those whom We guided and selected. When the verses of the All-Merciful were recited to them, they fell to the ground, bowing down and weeping.* (Quran, 19:58)

There are other believers whose souls falter in upholding their covenant with God, but who realize their shortcomings and repent to Him, seeking His pardon and forgiveness. These men and women reclaim a consciousness of their true human natures and acknowledge that they belong to God and to Him is their ultimate destiny. God has prepared for them delight, peace, fulfillment, and joy that never end:

> *Those who repent and believe and do righteous deeds, they shall enter the Garden—and they shall not be wronged in anything—Gardens of Eden, which the All-Merciful has promised His servants in the unseen. Indeed, it is He whose promise ever comes true. They shall not hear therein idle talk, but only, "Peace." And for them shall be their provision therein, morning and evening. This is the Garden which We shall give as inheritance to those of Our servants who are God-fearing.* (Quran, 19:60–63)

God's mercy is manifest. And His promise and warnings are unambiguous, especially regarding the ignoble destiny of those who reject faith and advocate perpetual skepticism and doubt as guides. They deny the existence of God or assign false gods or attributes with Him. They grow arrogant in the land, spread corruption, and wrong their fellow human beings. The end of all of these is made well known: *We but number for them a determined number ˹of days and deeds, until˺ the Day We assemble the God-fearing before the All-Merciful in honored delegations and drive the trespassers to Hell in droves* (Quran, 19:84–86).

This sets down the mission of the Quran: To transport this human creature beyond the limits of its clay form to the eternal and godly vision to which it is clearly called. It is a vision that has been infused within every man and woman. Neither the powers of the human senses nor the genius of empirical methods can accomplish this extraordinary task of true enlightenment. Attainment of knowledge such as this—a wisdom so transcending and a civility so fine that it uplifts man to a standing above the angelic—requires nothing less than the illumination of the human soul by the miraculous touch and mercy of God's revelation: *Thus We have indeed made ˹this Quran˺ easy in your tongue, for you to give glad tidings with it to the God-fearing and to warn therewith a contentious people* (Quran, 19:97).

PREFACE NOTES

1. John Polkinghorne, *Beyond Science: A Wider Context*, Cambridge University Press, 1998.
2. Francis Collins, director of the National Human Genome Research Institute, "Slate Magazine," June 2000.

INTRODUCTION

Mary in the Quran: A Model for Believers

The family of Mary, the mother of Jesus ﵇, enjoys a special and prominent place in Islam. The Quran's third chapter, one of the longest, is in fact named after this family (Âl ᶜImrân, or the Family of Amram). Throughout the Quran and in the teachings of the Prophet Muḥammad ﷺ there are references to Mary and to other members of her family. Along with the Quran's common reference to her as the mother of Jesus ﵇, it also identifies Mary as *the daughter of ᶜImrân* (Quran, 66:12), *sister of Aaron* (Quran, 19:28), and *she who preserved her chastity* (Quran, 21:91). We know from the teachings of Prophet Muḥammad ﷺ that John (Yaḥya ﵇) was Mary's nephew, that is, the son of her sister, thus making Zachariah ﵇ Mary's brother-in-law.[1] Hence, the Quran makes specific mention of Mary's father, ᶜImrân, and of Mary's mother, the wife of ᶜImrân (though the Quran does not mention her name). It is also possible that the reference to Mary as the *sister of Aaron* is literal, meaning that she had a brother named Aaron,[2] who then would be ʿImrân's son. This is, of course, in addition to ʿImrân's two daughters, Mary and the mother of John, as well as his two prophet grandsons, John عليه السلام and Jesus عليه السلام. This indeed constitutes distinguished recognition of one family, having only one parallel in the Quran, namely, the family of Abraham عليه السلام, his sons, grandchildren, and great grandchildren.

The family of ʿImrân, then, was truly exalted above much of humanity. Its members were luminaries of faith who devoted themselves to God and to consummate worship of Him: *God has surely chosen Adam and Noah, and the Family of Abraham and the Family of ʿImrân above all the worlds; ˹they were˺ descendants, one of another. And God is all-hearing, all-knowing* (Quran, 3:33–34). The Quran, however, gives particular distinction to Mary, even in the context of her eminent family, exalting her above all of them with the exception of her son Jesus عليه السلام, a fact reflected in the Quran's extended treatment of her life, available in no other scripture.

The story of Mary begins when her mother discovers that she herself is with child. Hopeful of giving birth to the prophet-heir of her people, she dedicates her unborn child (whom she anticipates to be a male) to the service of God throughout his life: *Behold, the wife of ʿImrân said, "My Lord, I have dedicated to You, in devotion, what is in my belly. So accept it from me. Indeed, You are the All-Hearing, the All-Knowing"* (Quran, 3:35). Mary's mother is taken aback, however, at the birth of a girl: *So when she delivered her, she said, "My Lord, indeed I have delivered her, a female"—and God knows best what she delivered—"and the male is not like the female!"* (Quran, 3:36). This last remark (*"the male is not like the female"*) is in reference to the office of prophethood being a male province, as was the traditional lifestyle of spiritual retreat among the Children of Israel. Yet the mother of Mary remains unswerving in her original consecration of the newborn, that Mary will serve the Sacred House even though she is a female. Mary is the recipient of her mother's deep affection and is named by her mother: *"And I have named her Mary. And I seek refuge in You for her and her children from Satan, the accursed"* (Quran, 3:36). God answers the wife of ʿImrân's plea: *Thus her Lord accepted 'Mary' with a good acceptance* (Quran, 3:37), and therewith commences the miracle-filled life of one of the most outstanding women in human history.

The Significance of Mary's Mention in the Quran

Whenever the Quran singles out someone by name, there is a far-reaching purpose for this that exceeds mere information.[3] The Quran mentions many women by title or reference—the wives of Adam, Noah, Lot, Pharaoh, and ʿImrân, for example; as well as the leader of Sheba (popularly known as the "Queen of Sheba" or Balqîs). It also mentions the "mother" and "sister" of Moses. But Mary is the only woman the Quran calls by her given name. This identification, coupled with the fact that the Quran highlights the nobility of Mary's genealogy, is a direct response to those who would accuse Mary of conceiving Jesus illicitly. God's specific and unambiguous reference to Mary in the Quran (and the narrative of the Annunciation and Immaculate Conception) is intended to leave no room for doubt or slanderous interpretation regarding the circumstances of Jesus' miraculous birth.

Mary's noble lineage and personal history, moreover, highlight the utter improbability of someone of Mary's distinction perpetrating a deed so decidedly beneath her station, as well as emphasizing her preeminent selection to receive the honor of giving birth to the Messiah. So central to the religious life of the Holy Land in Palestine is Mary's family that when the guardianship of Mary in the Sacred House is to be determined, the men of religion resolutely contend for this privilege (Quran, 3:44). Unable to come to consensus, they cast their scholarly pens as lots (some say into a river, to sink or float) in order to determine which of them would gain the honor of Mary's trusteeship. The distinction falls, by God's will, to Zachariah, the prophet among them. He then becomes responsible for the upbringing and education of his sister-in-law, as well as her spiritual and physical well-being: *Thus her Lord accepted her with a good acceptance and made her to grow a good growing, and He gave Zachariah the care of her* (Quran, 3:37).

Mary's devotion to God, even before her conception of Jesus, is pristine and total, and God's care for her is wondrous. She dwells in a cloistered chamber of the Sanctuary, dedicated to prayer and to the remembrance and contemplation of God. To all who behold her state of grace and piety, she is astonishing. No sustenance does she need but that it comes to her. No goodness does she find but that she attributes it to God's decree. No manifestation of blessing upon her appears but that she invokes God's limitless will and munificence:

> *Whenever Zachariah entered upon her in the Sanctuary, he found provisions by her. He said, "O Mary, from where does this come to you?" She said, "It is from God. Indeed, God gives provision to whomever He will without measure."* (Quran, 3:37)

Mary's reply thoroughly evinces her exceptional spiritual nurturing and deep-seated devotion. The proof that a spirit is indeed as radiant as this indicates lies in its ingenuous ability to kindle in a like fashion the spirits of others who come into its presence, a quality the Quran shows resident in Mary.

When Zachariah witnesses God's wonderful nurture of Mary, and the sight of his tender ward so faithfully dependent upon her Lord, he is immediately and wisely moved to ask God for the hidden desire of his own heart: To beget a pure and devout son, though his wife is barren and he is agèd: *Then and there, Zachariah called upon his Lord* (Quran, 3:38), and God answers his prayer in a prelude to the Annunciation to Mary of her conception of Jesus:

> *Angels called out to ˹Zachariah˺ as he stood praying in the Sanctuary, "God indeed gives you glad tidings of John ˹who shall be your son˺, confirming a word from God; ˹and he shall be˺ honorable and abstinent and a prophet from among the righteous."* (Quran, 3:39)

In Mary's case, the miracle would be even more wondrous. Here also God's angels usher Mary across the preternatural divide between the perceptible world and the unseen. It is through the angels that God prepares Mary's psychology to receive her momentous mission: *And behold, the angels said, "O Mary, indeed God has chosen you and purified you and has chosen you above the women of the world"* (Quran, 3:42).

The ordeal that Mary was about to face—the lonely anguish of an exceptional pregnancy and the terrible accusations of her own people—could only be endured by a soul that had been spiritually trained by steadfast, rigorous, and loving worship of God. Her steady, patient craft of prayer and contemplation, her reverence and purpose throughout the days and nights of her life—this had been Mary's gradual preparation for this momentous event: *"O Mary, have reverence for your Lord and bow down ˹to Him˺; and bow with those who bow"*

(Quran, 3:43). Moreover, human intelligence throughout the ages would not be prepared to accept the historical veracity of Mary's miracle from a less wholesome personage of lower ancestry. (Perhaps it is because of the popular effacing of Mary's religious experience, her remarkable spiritual constitution, and her hallowed family tree that the Immaculate Conception is increasingly viewed as merely a metaphor among modernist Christians.)

Thus the Quran follows up its account of Mary's eminence with a chastening reminder meant to keep in check the human propensity for speculation. The fact remains that none of us is in a position to know anything of the unseen and of the distant unrecorded past save what God Himself reveals. God says: *This is of the tidings of the unseen We reveal to you, ˹O Muḥammad˺. And you were not with them when they were casting their quills ˹to determine˺ which of them would have the care of Mary. And you were not with them when they were contending* (Quran, 3:44). In addition, the Prophet ﷺ, in more than one statement, underscored Mary's superior excellence, indicating that she was indeed among the foremost women who ever lived and will be among the most honored in Paradise.[4]

The Annunciation and Mary's Delivery of Jesus

In two places the Quran recounts the moment when Mary passes from wondrous child to miracle-filled woman.[5] In the first instance, the Quran reveals that a plurality of angels came to her with the announcement:[6]

> *Behold, the angels said, "O Mary, indeed God gives you glad tidings of a word from Him; his name is the Messiah, son of Mary, eminent in this world and the Hereafter and he is of those drawn near. And he shall*

speak to people in the cradle and as a grown man, and he shall be of the righteous." (Quran, 3:45–46)

This "word" is Jesus ﵇, and he is ennobled with the title the Messiah, or the Anointed one. He is called the son of Mary, rather than the common paternal reference, for he is to be without father, though he is purely human—flesh of her flesh. And his renown will be celebrated for all time.

The Quran records Mary's shock at what the angels proclaim. The living implications of the angels' pronouncement stun her. Standing suddenly at the nexus of the tangible world and the realm of the unseen, Mary is momentarily at a loss to comprehend: *She said, "My Lord, how shall I have a son while no human being has touched me?" He said, "So shall it be! God creates whatever He wills. When He decrees a matter, He but says to it 'Be!' and so it is"* (Quran, 3:47). Mary's assertion is silenced at the finality of God's irrepressible will. The angels then comfort her and confirm for her that her son shall be none other than the long-awaited prophet. Mary's baby will be God's chosen emissary to the Children of Israel whom they had been expecting. God will teach him the divine guidance so that he would walk in God's way, revive the truth of the Torah, and convey to the Children of Israel a new revelation from God: *And He shall teach him the Book and the wisdom and the Torah and the Evangel. And he is a messenger to the Children of Israel* (Quran, 3:48–49).

The Quran's second recital of the Annunciation, in Sûrat Maryam, is told more from the standpoint of Mary herself. It begins with Mary having retired from her people to a place that is described relative to her family's dwelling: *And mention in the Book Mary when she withdrew from her family to an eastern place* (Quran, 19:16). It is reasonable to conclude that the purpose of the retreat was for intensive spiritual solitude: *And she placed a veil between herself and them* (Quran, 19:17). During her seclusion God sends to her His foremost emissary, Angel Gabriel ﷺ, whose title is simply "the Spirit." He comes in the form of a man: *Then We sent to her Our Spirit, who thus appeared to her as a flawless human being* (Quran, 19:17). Struck with fear, Mary invokes God's protection and appeals to the stranger's sense of piety: *She said, "I seek refuge in the All-Merciful from you, if ever you were God-fearing!"* (Quran, 19:18). Gabriel then divulges his true identity and the matter for which he has come.

The message of the angels in the previous narration emphasizes the commanding power of God's will. Angel Gabriel's pronouncement articulates the notion of purity: *He said, "Indeed, I am none other than a messenger of your Lord, to grant to you a boy, ˹most˺ pure"* (Quran, 19:19). And like his mother, Mary's son is to be pure; and the nature of the conception will be immaculate. Yet this is Mary's moment of disorientation. It is the unanticipated command from the unseen and its effect in material flesh. In the heralding of Jesus' conception, we see Mary clinging to her faultless ethic of purity and chastity: *She said, "How can I have a boy while no human being has touched me, nor have I been unchaste?"* (Quran, 19:20).

But such notions were of this world, and it is Mary's innocence and her developed God-consciousness that make her worthy of the miracle of the Immaculate Conception. For the son of Mary is forever to be a portent to humankind that God's will is indomitable, that God's divinity is unrivaled and unshared—no matter the miracles He creates on earth for human eyes: *He said, "So shall it be! Your Lord has said, 'It is easy for Me. And We shall make him a sign for all people, and a mercy from Us—and it is a matter decreed'"* (Quran, 19:21).

The Quran does not detail how the conception of Jesus occurred, nor does it specify the term of pregnancy, though some hold that the gestation was extraordinary in its brevity. Yet the Quran does tell of Mary again situating herself far from her people after her conception: *So she conceived him and withdrew with him to a remote place* (Quran, 19:22). She is alone when destiny overtakes her, and she takes relief against a tree: *And the birth pangs drove her to the trunk of a date-palm* (Quran, 19:23). Without husband and in the throes of labor—mortified by the accusations and terrible glances that will surely be directed toward her—Mary breaks down and bewails her outcast state. She pleads to God, the Lord of Time, that He send her into oblivion so that she could never be a memory to anyone: *She said, "Oh, woe to me! If only I had died before this and become something utterly forgotten!"* (Quran, 19:23).

Yet this is a place to which the Quran has taken us before. A cry goes forth from a faithful servant and God fulfills the need. But perhaps no moment in history is more enchanted than the instant of Mary's anguished delivery of Jesus عليه السلام:

> *Then he*[7] *called to her from beneath her, "Do not sorrow. Assuredly your Lord has placed beneath you a streamlet. And shake toward you the trunk of the date-palm, and it shall drop upon you dates, ripe and fresh. So eat and drink and cool your eyes. And if you should see any human being, then say, 'Indeed, I have vowed to the All-Merciful a fast. Thus never shall I speak today to any human being.'"* (Quran, 19:24–26)

The spurting of the rivulet from the earth beneath her, the lush fruition of the date-palm, and especially the miraculous speech of her newborn comfort Mary. God's will to unmistakably bestow upon His emissary miraculous portents confirms the truthfulness and prophethood of Jesus. This has now been fully demonstrated to Mary. Moreover, she knows that God's loving succor throughout her life and in the hour of her distress has been unfailing. She has been chosen, and God's will shall be done. Her test would now be upon every other. No longer would she fret over sin and insult. For the task of Mary's defense, by God's will, would be taken up by the newborn himself.

Replenished, Mary returns to her people openly, with her swaddled and pure son. Aghast in disbelief at what their eyes behold—their unwed daughter of the chosen family presenting them with her own child—Mary's people lash out:

> *Then she came with him to her people, carrying him. They said, "O Mary! Truly you have come with something unimaginable! O sister of Aaron, your father was not an evil person, nor was your mother unchaste."* (Quran, 19:27–28)

Maintaining her vow not to speak, Mary confidently gestures to her family to seek out their queries from the baby. Taunted by the absurdity of the suggestion, they respond with utter dismay: *They said, "How shall we speak to one in the cradle, an infant boy?"* (Quran, 19:29). With the audible and intelligible speech of a baby in a cradle, their outrage is quelled and their emotion dissolved into the realization that God is, indeed, all-creating and all-knowing, and that a miracle had occurred:

> *'Jesus' said, "Indeed, I am the servant of God. He has given me the Book and has made me a prophet. And He has made me blessed wherever I may be; and He has enjoined upon me the Prayer and Charity, as long as I am alive, and being virtuous to my mother; and He has not made me insolent, wretched. So peace be upon me the day I was born, and the day I die, and the day I am raised to life."* (Quran, 19:30–33)

There is no thought among Mary's people of any confusion

between the identities of Jesus 🕊️ and God. Never did this unconventional conception cause Mary's family to become unfamiliar with the original and eternal commandment of God: *Indeed, I am God! There is no God but I. So worship Me.* (Quran, 20:14). Such dissensions arose slowly over generations, only after Jesus' equally miraculous departure from the earth (just as defiance and false attributions had ensued regarding others before him). Therein resides the answer to their perennial self-questioning: *Who is Jesus and who is God?*

> *That is Jesus, son of Mary, the word of truth, about whom they bitterly contend. It is not for God to take a son. Glory be to Him! When He decrees a matter, He but says to it "Be!" and so it is. "And indeed, God is my Lord and your Lord; so worship Him. This is a straight way."*[II]
> (Quran, 19:34–36)

INTRODUCTION NOTES

1. In his miraculous Night Journey from Makkah to Jerusalem and subsequent ascension to Heaven, the Prophet 🕊️ said that he saw Jesus 🕊️ and John 🕊️ together in the second heaven. He described them as "two sons of maternal aunts," that is, of sisters. See *Ṣaḥīḥ Muslim* ("The Book of Faith"), *ḥadīth* number 259.

2. Some commentators consider the mention of the name Aaron to be an allusion to Aaron the prophet 🕊️, brother of Moses 🕊️, in which case it could be taken as an indication that Mary descend-

ed from the line of Aaron among the Children of Israel. Such commentators sometimes take the ʿImrân (Amram) of the Quran to be, not Mary's actual father, but the father of Moses ﷺ and Aaron ﷺ, who is also said to have been named ʿImrân. Others, like al-Ṭabarî, state that Mary is a descendent of the line of David ﷺ, for which there seems to be corroboration in biblical accounts indicating that the Children of Israel anticipated the Messiah from the line of David ﷺ. There is implication in the statements of the Prophet Muḥammad ﷺ that the Aaron mentioned in association with Mary was, indeed, a prominent man of her time, who was named after his illustrious ancestor. This could also serve to strengthen the opinion that the ʿImrân mentioned straightforwardly in the Quran as Mary's father (66:12) was, indeed, her actual father, named after his noble ancestor. It is reported in several *ḥadîth* collections, including those of Muslim, Tirmidhî, Nisâʾî, and Aḥmad, that al-Mughîra ibn Shuʿbah related the following:

> The Messenger of God ﷺ sent me to the people of Najrân, and they said, "Have you considered what you have recited to us ˹from the Quran; namely, the phrase˺ 'O Sister of Aaron,' while Moses came before Jesus in such and such?" When I returned, I mentioned this to the Messenger of God ﷺ, who said, "Did you not inform them that they used to name after the prophets and the righteous before them?" (Zuḥaylî, *Tafsîr al-Munîr*, Part 16, p. 82).

For more on this topic, see the Appendix "Daughter of ʿImrân."

3. See my book *Father of the Flame*, p. 4, in which I speak about God mentioning Abû Lahab by name.

4. *Ṣaḥîḥ al-Bukhârî*, 3411 and 3432. *Ṣaḥîḥ Muslim*, 2431.

5. The verse, *And ˹behold˺ Mary, daughter of ʿImrân, who preserved her chastity. Then We breathed into her of Our spirit. And she confirmed the word of her Lord and His books. And she was ever of those who are reverential* (Quran, 66:12), also refers to the event of the Annunciation.

6. Some commentators, like al-Ṭabarî (3:268–74) and Ibn Kathîr (p.

834), surmise that this visitation of the angels to Mary was a preliminary one, preparing her for the visit of the Angel Gabriel عليه السلام (as described in Sûrat Maryam 19:17–21). They hold that it was Gabriel عليه السلام who announced to Mary the actual conception of Jesus عليه السلام and who administered the miracle. This suggests that the weightiness of Mary's mission—miraculously conceiving and giving birth to a child without a father, who was, moreover, the promised Messiah, and among the most significant human beings in history—would require of Mary time for reflection in order for her to summon the necessary resolve.

7. The word "he" in this verse refers to Jesus. But, according to many commentators, it may instead refer to the angel of annunciation, that is, Gabriel.

8. The speaker of this quote may be either Jesus, showing what he had preached to his people, or the Prophet Muḥammad, reinforcing what all the prophets had said.

OVERVIEW

SÛRAT MARYAM: CONTEXT AND THEMES

Sûrat Maryam is the nineteenth chapter of the Quran and takes its name from Mary and the account of her miraculous conception and delivery of Jesus عليه السلام. Among the most remarkable narratives in all history, this story is told from verses 16 to 36 of this sura (as well as in other passages of the Quran). The sura is also known by the five "opening" or "disconnected" letters of its first verse, *kâf, hâ, yâ, ʿayn, ṣâd* [كهيعص].

Sûrat Maryam was revealed to the Prophet Muḥammad ﷺ in Makkah in the fourth year of his prophethood, immediately before the emigration of a company of Muslims to Africa so as to escape the persecution of the Qurayshite disbelievers. The exodus served also to introduce the message of Islam outside the Arabian Peninsula. More specifically, it began Islam's dialogue with another faith community, that of the Christian kingdom of Abyssinia (modern day Ethiopia), ruled by the just sovereign al-Najâshî, known also by the Latinate title the Negus.

Sûrat Maryam succeeded the revelation of Sûrat Fâṭir (the Quran's thirty-fifth chapter) and preceded Sûrat Ṭâ Hâ (the twentieth chapter). It was the first sura in the chronology of the Quran's revelation to present the narrative of Mary and to affirm her eminent rank. The unity of its style, in addition to the context of its revelation, substantiates the well-founded opinion that God revealed all of Sûrat Maryam to the Prophet ﷺ at one time.[1]

The name "Maryam" (Mary) occurs thirty-four times in the Quran, eleven instances of which occur in contexts that assert her nobility, which include the mention of God's favor upon her and the Annunciation regarding her conception of Jesus. The Quran also makes an allusion to Mary by way of her elevated character: *And ⌜behold the excellence of⌝ she who preserved her chastity: Thus We breathed into her of Our spirit, and We made her and her son a sign for all the worlds* (Quran, 21:91). The remaining instances mention Mary's name by way of attributing Jesus' parentage to her alone, as in the phrase "Jesus, son of Mary."

Jews, Christians, and Pagans in Arabia

The Arabian Peninsula takes its name from the tribal Arabs that have inhabited its desert landscapes since antiquity and who have consistently comprised the great majority of its population. Long before Islam, the Arabs fell from the path of their forefathers Abraham عليه السلام and Ishmael عليه السلام and followed chiefly pagan religions. Eventually, a number of tribes converted to Christianity: The Banû Taghlib, who inhabited northern Arabia near what is present-day Iraq; the Ghassânids, who neighbored the Roman-occupied territory to the northwest; and the clans of Najrân, who formed a sizable Christian community in the south. In addition, several Jewish tribes migrated to live among the Arabs in Western Arabia, known as the Ḥijâz specifically in Khaybar, Fadak, and Yathrib (named later as Madinah, the city of the Prophet ﷺ). Jewish tribes also lived in Yemen, at the southwest point of the peninsula, separated from the Horn of Africa by a thin strip of the Red Sea.

Though religion and geography drew lines between tribes and peoples, the Arabic tongue prevailed among them—not only as the language of daily use, but as an idiom of culture, moored especially in poetic expression and generations of shared memory. So it was Arabic, informed by a severe region that tended toward isolation, that held the tribes of Arabia in loose constellation. Ibn Khaldûn, the preeminent Arab historian (d. 1406), makes the point that while the Jewish and Christian tribes of Arabia adhered to their faiths, neither really possessed more than a simple awareness of their religions. He said, "The adherents of the Torah who lived among the Arabs ˹prior to Islam˺ were Bedouins like ˹their Arab counterparts˺ and knew of ˹the Torah˺ only what the common People of the Book knew."[2] The absence of any city of religious illumination (for the People of the Book) in the Arabian Peninsula centuries before the advent of Islam confirms his observation; for certainly the Christians and the Jews incorporated prominent centers of learning wherever they flourished, as in Babylon, Antioch, Palestine, Alexandria, Rome, and other such places.

Still, the effect of this diversity within such stark, homogenizing conditions was to prepare pre-Islamic Arabia as an arena of religious discourse between Jewish, Christian, and pagan Arab tribes. In this crucible, the great religious issues were vitalized: Belief in the oneness of God; the attribution of sons, daughters, and other entities to Him; the recognition of the office of prophethood; and the awareness that they were eligible, according to lineage and prophecy, to witness the choice of such a man by God. Thus there existed among the peoples of Arabia the notion of revealed scriptures that God sent down to communities to establish among them the tenets and laws that inform a godly way of life. No matter how rudimentary, it was nevertheless understood in much of the Arabian context that only under the auspices of the heavenly Books, like that given to their forefather Abraham عليه السلام, could morality and ethical norms be mutually accepted and established such that man's covenant with God could be fulfilled. Naturally, the People of the Book, the Jews and the Christians, enjoyed a certain prestige above the Arab pagans because (as their designation indicates) they were recipients of a revealed scripture, namely; the Torah (*Tawrât*) of Moses عليه السلام and the Evangel, or Gospel, (*Injîl*) of Jesus عليه السلام.

The Arabs, however, were acutely aware that the People of the Book disputed among themselves about the most primary religious issues, and thus the vast majority of Arabs would follow neither the Jews nor the Christians, but rather viewed them with a mixture of reproof and apprehension. This is borne out by an authentic report about the Arabs in Yathrib that explains their eagerness to respond to the call of Muḥammad ﷺ. Whenever tensions mounted between them and their Jewish neighbors, the Jews would threaten the Arabs with a prophecy from their scripture that indicated a prophet from the line of Abraham was to appear in Arabia. They would say, "With him we will slaughter you as ʿÂd and Iram (two ancient Arab tribes) were destroyed by God before."

The picture of seventh-century Arabia that emerges, then, is one of a society in flux: The contrary forces of an elaborately developed code of tribalism were furrowing deeper while distinctions between groups and classes were growing sharper. At the same time, the Arabic language and a severe natural environment induced a commonality and interconnectedness in Arabian life. Closer scrutiny of the Arabian mosaic, however, shows that the controlling principles of disparity that dictated culture and prevented Arabia's ascent to civilization were anchored, not merely in tribalism, but in the skewed religious viewpoints that ultimately verified the tribal outlook. For though the peoples of Arabia accepted in principle the primacy of heavenly revelation, in actuality no existing message could avail itself of that lofty status. Sectarian disputes, ancestral hostility, and the consequent confusion among the People of the Book rendered their claims to divine guidance ineffective because it subordinated their transcendent messages to a socially disintegrative parochialism. Meanwhile, the tribal elite among the pagan Arabs were only too happy to go on unencumbered by a revelation. The brutal status quo of Arabian life afforded them advantages that they would never give over freely.

This was the Arabian context that the revelation of the Quran altered—a circumstance that we may better understand after examining the barriers that separated the Jews, the Christians, and the pagan Arabs.

Religious Partisanship in Pre-Islamic Arabia

Abraham عليه السلام was the common patriarch of Arabia's Jews, Christians, and idolaters, but clashing beliefs reinforced by fierce tribal loyalties deeply divided his descendants. The Jews refused to acknowledge Jesus عليه السلام as the prophet-heir sent to the Children of Israel after Moses عليه السلام. They condemned his birth as the outcome of an immoral failing on the part of his mother, Mary. So the Jewish tribes persisted in their contention that they awaited the promised Messiah and that Jesus عليه السلام was not the one foretold. No reported miracle by which God confirmed Jesus عليه السلام as the Messiah—neither his healing of the blind and the leper, his breathing of life into a clay figure of a bird, his raising of the dead, nor other God-given miracles—proved sufficient to them that Jesus عليه السلام was, indeed, a true prophet. Instead, they viewed him as a rebel who violated the sacred law of the Torah and the covenant of the Children of Israel.

The Christians accepted Jesus عليه السلام as the Messiah and believed that his message came from God. They revered him enormously and acknowledged that Mary had indeed safeguarded her virginity and had delivered Jesus into the world by way of a divine miracle. They developed beliefs, however, that his miraculous birth without a father—corroborated by the stunning miracles he performed—was proof that he was the divine "son" of God, and that he himself was the Lord.

The Arab pagans, who constituted the great majority of the Peninsula's populace, claimed to follow the way of Abraham عليه السلام. Yet there was an absence of credible texts of their own that would substantiate and codify their religious practices. What the Quran records of the pre-Islamic Arabs' beliefs and customs outlines the essential features of their religion. The Arabs believed in a chief God who generated the existence of the world: *And if you were to ask them, "Who created the heavens and the earth, and subjugated the sun and the moon?" they would surely say, "God!"* (Quran, 29:61). Alongside God, however, they embraced a multitude of idols and images that they took as associate-gods and through whom they sought divine intercession:

> *Most surely, to God alone belongs the pure religion. Yet those who have taken patrons apart from Him 'say': "We do not worship them except that they may draw us near to God in subservient status." Indeed, God shall judge between them about that in which they are disputing.* (Quran, 39:3)

Furthermore, paganism was well suited to assimilating the Arabs' ardent desires and biases into its polytheistic world view. Thus the pre-Islamic Arabs, notorious in their desire to beget sons and in their shame at having daughters, nevertheless claimed that the angels were the "daughters of God," a contradiction for which the Quran roundly ridiculed them. *Moreover, they attribute daughters to God—Glory be to him!—yet for themselves is whatever 'gender' they desire!* (Quran, 16:57). They established, moreover, kinship between God and the jinn.[3] *And they appointed for God associate-gods from among the jinn, though He created them* (Quran, 6:100).

The many accounts that have reached us about pre-Islamic Arab religious practice augment the statements of the Quran and illustrate just how prolific and pervasive Arab idolatry was. Not only did it misconstrue and mingle the worship of God with false deities, but also it encompassed the random worship of natural and man-made objects. One Companion of the Prophet ﷺ related the following anecdote:

> In the period of religious ignorance before Islam, whenever we came across a nice stone we worshipped it. When we found none, we used to heap up a small mound of sand then bring a camel and milk it over the sand heap. Then we would worship 'the mound' or circumambulate it for as long as we remained there.[4]

Another of the Companions recounted with humor, "My family once sent me with a goblet full of milk and butter to their gods. I wanted to taste the butter, but I refrained because I feared the gods. Then a dog came and ate the butter, drank the milk, and urinated on the idols ˹known as˺ Isâf and Nâ'ilah."[5]

In the same vein, it is said that the famed Arab poet Umru' al-Qays once sought guidance from an idol as to the course of action he should take in avenging the killing of his father. As was the practice of the people in such cases, he brought divining rods with him to the idol in order to discern whether or not he should retaliate. Yet each time he raised the question and threw down the rods, their pattern indicated that he should not retaliate, until in frustration he broke the rods and struck the face of the idol with them, saying, "Bite the buttocks of your father! Had it been *your* father who was slain, you would not prevent me." Then he sought to avenge his father's killing.[6]

The pagan Arabs also rejected the tenet of belief in the Hereafter, finding the notion of resurrection and life after death implausible. The Quran records their mockery of the Hereafter: *They said, "When we are dead and we have become dust and bones, shall we indeed be raised to life? Truly, we have already been promised this—we and our forefathers of old. Indeed, this is nothing but fables of the ancients!"* (Quran, 23:82–83). The Quran addresses this skepticism in Sûrat Maryam, and in many other places: *Man says, "Is it that when I have died, I shall ˹again˺ be brought forth alive?" Does man not remember that We indeed created him before, and he ˹once˺ was nothing?* (Quran, 19:66–67).

The Quran also points out that before the advent of Islam, the Arab pagans had been sharply critical of both the Jews and the Christians for allowing a chasm to spread between them and divine guidance:

> *And they swore by God, with the utmost of their vows, that if there came to them a ˹prophetic˺ warner they would most surely be the most guided of any one of the communities. Yet when there came to them a warner, it did nothing but increase them in aversion ˹and in˺ arrogance in the land and evil plotting.* (Quran, 35:42–43)

In the context of this stalemate Sûrat Maryam was revealed. It addressed the religious disputation that had embroiled the past faith communities and uttered the last word on the crucial issues concerning ultimate human destiny. As a revelation, it presented the position of Islam on the specific matters and key personalities (specifically, Mary and Jesus) around which great religious dispute raged (and still does to this day). It also delimits for Muslims the proper scope of their dialogue with the People of the Book and with those who worship idols or disbelieve in God altogether. In addition, its very revelation signaled a deliberate widening of the substance and the field of Islam's discourse.

Sûrat Maryam in the Vista of the Abyssinian Christian Kingdom

In the early years of his mission, the Prophet ﷺ faced a near total rejection of his message from the Makkan chieftains—the social, tribal, and commercial elite of Quraysh. The sophistication and character of the assault waged against the Prophet ﷺ and against the poor, the unprotected, and the women who followed him are eye opening. The Quraysh's psychological, economic, and physical persecutions were an attempt to abort the new religion, to turn back to idolatry those who embraced Islam's defining beliefs—there is no deity other than

God, and Muḥammad is the Messenger of God—and to deter anyone who inclined toward the Prophet's message.

After five years of intense oppression, a company of Muslim men and women, at the bidding of the Prophet ﷺ, secretly departed for Abyssinia in search of asylum and religious liberty in this Christian kingdom. They departed in two groups, the first a band of fifteen and the second a group of eighty-three men and women. At their head was Jaᶜfar, the Prophet's cousin and the son of the pagan but sympathetic uncle of the Prophet ﷺ, Abû Ṭâlib. It is said that Jaᶜfar closely resembled the Prophet ﷺ in appearance and character. There in Abyssinia, Jaᶜfar would make one of history's most eloquent stands for freedom of religion and witness one of Islam's most gallant successes.

Historians and biographers of the life of the Prophet ﷺ differ about the motives behind the Abyssinian migration. The majority of them explain that its main impetus was to flee Makkan persecution. In light of the chronology of the Quran's revelation, however, it is worthy to point out that persecution was probably not the sole consideration for the emigration; perhaps it was not even the major reason underlying it. Passages of the Quran that were revealed before Sûrat Maryam show a steady amplification of Islam's universal voice, a deliberate direction to lift the new religion to a global, civilizational level.

The Quran increasingly spoke of God, not only as the Creator, but as *the Lord of the Worlds* (Quran, 1:2) and as *the Lord of all people, King of all people, God of all people* (Quran, 114:1–3). And God Himself described the Quran as *the Criterion,* that is, a new scripture that was to be the religious standard, the ethical measure by which humankind was to live and be guided. God said, moreover, that He sent it down *upon His servant,* Muḥammad ﷺ, whom He commissioned *to be a warner*—not merely for the Arabs or the seventh century—*but for [all] the worlds* (Quran, 25:1). The Quran had begun to openly speak of itself as *a reminder to the worlds* (Quran, 38:87, 68:52), alerting humanity that *you shall assuredly know its tidings after a time* (Quran, 38:88).

The Quran's universal address preceded the Abyssinian migration, which indicates that to live Islam's way of life free of an Arabian pagan milieu was a main objective of this ten-year episode, and to find peaceful coexistence with a Christian society was another. For in such an environment Muslims could feel secure in adhering to the principles of their religion and worship, albeit with religious differences between them and their neighbors. Muslims also would present a vibrant model of Islam's creed and morality in their new context. The People of the Book would learn firsthand that the essence of Islam was but a continuation of the message of the prophets of old—Noah, Abraham, Moses, and Jesus (peace be upon them)—with whom they were already familiar. This familiarization, in fact, occurred in the course of the Abyssinian migration.

Muslims lived among their Christian hosts in good faith. There came a time early on, however, when this mutual good will was tested. The Quraysh—who feared a loss of containment of Islam—sent emissaries to Abyssinia in an attempt to have the runaway Muslims extradited back into their hostile hands. They claimed that these Muslims were radical elements in rebellion against the long-established norms of Makkan society and that they shared no worthy commonality with the Christian community in the east African land. Having gained favor with many of the Abyssinian court ministers through largess, the Makkan emissaries effectively placed the fate of the Muslim émigrés in the hands of just one man, the Abyssinian king, al-Najâshî. There were alternative lands to which the Prophet ﷺ could have directed these fleeing Muslims, but he himself had selected Abyssinia, a Christian polity, and specifically this one because it was led by a man known for his integrity. In his own careful wording, the Prophet ﷺ said that this man was "a king under whose rule people were not oppressed."[7] The Prophet ﷺ must have perceived, at the very least, that God had prepared Muslims for an open dialogue with the Christian faith community, for prior to the revelation of Sûrat Maryam, such an engagement would not have been feasible and such a move to a Christian community would not have been secure. Ultimately, then, this sura proved to be the vital force that enabled the nascent Muslim community to migrate and, in the process, deliver a critical diplomatic blow to the Quraysh power elite.

According to Muslim historian Ibn Isḥâq (d. 151 H/768 CE), the Makkan emissaries, with the backing of the court bishops, appealed to al-Najâshî to remand the Muslim company into their custody, which he summarily refused without first hearing the stand of the Muslims. A Muslim delegation, with Jaʿfar ibn Abî Ṭâlib at its head, was summoned to the court to answer the charges. Jaʿfar stood before the king and the attendant bishops and defended the case of Islam and that of the believers. He said:

> O King, we were a people steeped in ignorance, worshipping idols, eating carrion, committing abominations, severing relations with kinship, and ill-treating our neighbors. The strong among us devoured the weak. This had been our way until God sent us a

> messenger from among ourselves. We know his lineage, his truthfulness, his trustworthiness, and his integrity. He called us to God—to believe in Him alone and worship Him—and to renounce what our fathers, and we, used to worship apart from Him, of stones and idols. He commanded us to speak the truth, fulfill trusts, be dutiful to kinship, be good to our neighbors, and to refrain from what is forbidden and from bloodshed. He has forbidden us from obscenities, from speaking falsehoods, from devouring the property of the orphan, and from vilifying virtuous women. He has commanded us to worship God alone, and never to associate anything with Him. And he has enjoined us to establish the Prayer, Charity, and Fasting. [Then Jaʿfar listed the tenets of Islam.]
>
> So we accepted his truth, and we have believed in him. And we have followed what he has brought from God. Thus we have worshipped God alone and we have not associated anything with Him. And we have held as forbidden what He has forbidden and as lawful what He has made lawful. Then our people turned against us, tormented us, and persecuted us, so that we may forsake our religion and revert back to the worship of idols instead of the worship of God, the Exalted, and that ˹we may indulge˺ in the evil deeds in which we once indulged. So when they oppressed us, treated us unjustly, and constrained our lives and denied us our religion, we came to your land and have chosen you above all others. And we are hopeful for your protection, and request that we not suffer injustice from you.

Thereafter Jaʿfar recited to al-Najâshî verses from Sûrat Maryam that tell of the miraculous birth of Jesus عليه السلام. The monarch said, "This has truly come from the same source as that which Jesus brought. . . .What do you say of Jesus?" Jaʿfar said, "We say of him what our Prophet brought to us, that he is the servant of God, and he is His messenger and His spirit and His word which He cast unto Mary, the virgin." Then al-Najâshî picked up a splinter of wood and said, "Jesus, the son of Mary, does not exceed what you have said by the length of this stick."[8]

A Thematic Outline of Sûrat Maryam

Sûrat Maryam touches on several principal issues of religion that the Quran as a whole details:

1. Belief in one God, who alone brings into existence whatever He wills in any way He wills, and that to Him is the ultimate destiny. He alone is the giver of provision, well-being, and, above all, divine guidance leading to faith and excellence in character and morality.
2. Belief in the messengers and the prophets of God as conveyers of divine guidance to humanity.
3. Belief in the unseen; namely, that part of creation that God has not made manifest to human beings. Belief in the existence of angels (and their ceaseless obedience to God), as well as belief in the existence of jinn, among whom is Satan, who is the avowed enemy of humankind, relentless in his striving to mislead people away from the straight way.
4. Belief in the decree of God, in a purposeful human existence, and in the ultimate destiny of humanity.
5. Belief in the Afterlife, in which everyone shall stand before God and be recompensed according to his or her belief and the deeds one has performed in this life.

Sûrat Maryam's treatment of these issues is condensed and illustrated. It amplifies an overriding theme of hope in the mercy of God. But it also admonishes those who choose flagrant disbelief and corruption. Herein, the sura shows two examples of people: First, the messengers, the prophets, and the believers from among the Children of Adam; and second, the disbelievers who reject faith in God and deny His emissaries, His revelation, and the Day of Judgment. The first fifty-eight verses of Sûrat Maryam identify a chain of exemplary role models. The passages recount the experiences of Zachariah and the birth of his son John (Quran, 19:2–15); of Mary and the birth of her son Jesus (Quran, 19:17–40); and of Abraham and, first, his encounter with his idol-worshipping father and, then, God's bestowal upon the great patriarch of worthy heirs: Isaac and Jacob (Quran, 19:41–50). Brief mention of Moses and Aaron (Quran, 19:51–53), Ishmael (Quran, 19:54–55), and Idrîs (Enoch) (Quran, 19:56–57) round out the sura's enunciation of messengers and prophets.

The sura then recalls the righteous seed of Adam and Noah, and again Abraham and Jacob, through whom God transported the prophets of humanity (Quran, 19:58). Here the Quran speaks of the grace that God bestowed upon these chosen ones, these guides and teachers to humanity (and their generations of followers), and of their loving worship of God. For not a sign of God was made manifest to them, but that they humbled themselves upon the earth and wept, awestruck before the towering mercy of their Lord (Quran, 19:58). The sura picks up this very theme in its closing verses, which address the Prophet Muḥammad ﷺ. God reminds him of His immense favor in making the Quran easy for his utterance and remembrance and in defining his prophetic mission as a warner and a bearer of glad tidings (Quran, 19:97).

In contrast to the prophets and the believers, Sûrat Maryam identifies generations of people who lived in the period between the cessation of prophethood among the Children of

Israel and the advent of Muḥammad ﷺ. These generations forsook the prescribed Prayer and took their whims as their guide. They were ultimately ruined (Quran, 19:59). The sura then presents a disbeliever (presumably a Makkan) who voices a typical rejection of the notion of resurrection after death. The Quran's response is a terrifying depiction of the state of these deniers on the Day of Resurrection (Quran, 19:66–72). In this life, the deniers took great pride in their wealth, prestige, and lineage, flaunting them as the criteria to claim superiority over those who believe (Quran, 19:73–76). The sura repudiates the conception that these fleeting things of life earn one special favor with God (Quran, 19:77–80). On the contrary, these disbelievers shall meet a most miserable end (Quran, 19:81–87). And the same holds true of those who allege that God has taken a son, for, no matter the intention, it is an attribution of a partner to God, thus violating the central truth of all being: God is One. Those who commit the abomination of ascribing a child to God, the Quran tells us, utter a sacrilege that the earth, the mountains, and the heavenly vault above reject with such vehemence that they nearly burst and collapse (Quran, 19:88–92).

Rather, Sûrat Maryam has been sent down to proclaim that nothing in all existence stands before God as other than His worshipper (Quran, 19:93–95). Then let those among the human family who willingly accept and excel in that worship and faith know that God, the All-Merciful, shall engender between them a special and pure love (Quran, 19:96).

OVERVIEW NOTES

1. This is contrary to the minority opinion that verses 58–59 were revealed in Madinah. See *al-Taḥrîr wa al-Tanwîr,* 16:58.

2. Ibn Khaldûn, *Muqaddima,* p. 555. (The translation here is my own. For further reading on this topic in English, one may see Franz Rosenthal's translation of the *Muqaddima,* 2:445.)

3. Jinn, angels, and human beings are intelligent creatures. God created angels from light, jinn from fire, and human beings from earth. Angels are obedient creatures who unfailingly carry out God's commands. Jinn, like human beings, have choice and free will. They are, therefore, subject to obligation by God and answerable to Him for their deeds, and God shall assemble them on the Day of Resurrection and recompense them with reward or punishment. Jinn, like angels, are invisible to human beings, yet they see us from where we do not see them (Quran, 7:27). While their creation predates that of humankind's, several verses of the Quran and a substantial number of verified statements of the Prophet ﷺ confirm that they too live on earth—eating, drinking, procreating, and dying—and that, like humans, they agree and disagree, choose belief or disbelief, and are charged with adhering to the religion of Islam. As the formation of jinn differs from that of humans, differences of nature arise, the pertinent consequences of which are several. In addition to normally being invisible to humans, jinn have the ability to travel vast distances in mere moments (Quran, 39:40); to pierce the earth's atmosphere and penetrate high into the heavens (Quran, 72:8–9); to assume, at times, animal or human forms; and to access human thought and introduce suggestions to it. The Quran states emphatically, however, that jinn—Satan being the chief of the disbelieving ones—possess no authority whatever over human beings. Their "power" is merely one of suggestion. Thus, whoever so elects may follow their evil suggestions, and he or she will bear full responsibility for this. Jinn may attempt to scare human beings (though they them-

selves may be frightened of some human believers). In any case, the Quran stresses the importance of seeking refuge in God from them and seeking protection against their evil doings (Quran, suras 113 and 114). See al-Ṭabarî, *Jâmiᶜ al-Bayân*, 7:514, 8:236, and 12:258–77.

4. Sunan al-Dârimî, 1:4.

5. Sunan al-Dârimî, 1:4.

6. *Al-Aṣnâm*, p. 47. See also, ᶜAbd al-Raḥmân ibn Yûsuf ibn ᶜIsâ al-Malâḥî, *Dawâfaᶜ Inkâr Daᶜwat al-Ḥaq fî al-Aḥd al-Nabawî wa Subul ᶜIlâjiha* (Riyâḍ: Dâr ᶜAlam al-Kutub, 1993), p. 105.

7. Ibn Hishâm, 1:280.

8. Ibn Hishâm, 1:290–91.

KEY TO THE "INTERLINEAR COMMENTARY"

The *colored italicized text* represents the close translation of the meaning of the revealed Arabic Quran. The word order of this *interpretation* has been retained in almost every case so that one can read it continuously to the exclusion of the surrounding text in order to glean the message of a verse more directly. The black roman-face text represents explanations that provide conceptual background and vital context based on authoritative commentaries and sound scholarship.

COMMENTARY

Sura 19

Maryam
MARY

I. Human Intention and Divine Intervention

سورة مريم

بسم الله الرحمن الرحيم

كهيعص ١

In the name of God, the All-Merciful, the Mercy-Giving.

(1) PRELUDE: CALLING TO MINDFULNESS

Kâf Hâ Yâ ᶜAyn Ṣâd 1

Listen to the revelation of God now being recited to you! It is composed of individual letters of the Arabic alphabet; yet it is inimitable. This Quran—its form, style, scope, and power to transform the human heart—is without compare in the ancient legacy of Arabic culture or in the history of human expression.

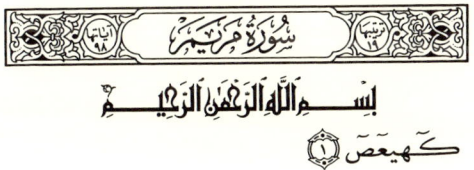

Hear, then, this Quran and learn from the struggles and wonders that have passed long before you, and know that the revealer of this Book is none other than the true and only God.

ذِكۡرُ رَحۡمَتِ رَبِّكَ عَبۡدَهُۥ زَكَرِيَّآ ٢
إِذۡ نَادَىٰ رَبَّهُۥ نِدَآءً خَفِيّٗا ٣ قَالَ رَبِّ إِنِّي وَهَنَ ٱلۡعَظۡمُ
مِنِّي وَٱشۡتَعَلَ ٱلرَّأۡسُ شَيۡبٗا وَلَمۡ أَكُنۢ بِدُعَآئِكَ رَبِّ
شَقِيّٗا ٤ وَإِنِّي خِفۡتُ ٱلۡمَوَٰلِيَ مِن وَرَآءِي وَكَانَتِ
ٱمۡرَأَتِي عَاقِرٗا فَهَبۡ لِي مِن لَّدُنكَ وَلِيّٗا ٥ يَرِثُنِي وَيَرِثُ
مِنۡ ءَالِ يَعۡقُوبَۖ وَٱجۡعَلۡهُ رَبِّ رَضِيّٗا ٦ يَٰزَكَرِيَّآ
إِنَّا نُبَشِّرُكَ بِغُلَٰمٍ ٱسۡمُهُۥ يَحۡيَىٰ لَمۡ نَجۡعَل لَّهُۥ مِن قَبۡلُ سَمِيّٗا
٧ قَالَ رَبِّ أَنَّىٰ يَكُونُ لِي غُلَٰمٞ وَكَانَتِ ٱمۡرَأَتِي
عَاقِرٗا وَقَدۡ بَلَغۡتُ مِنَ ٱلۡكِبَرِ عِتِيّٗا ٨ قَالَ كَذَٰلِكَ
قَالَ رَبُّكَ هُوَ عَلَيَّ هَيِّنٞ وَقَدۡ خَلَقۡتُكَ مِن قَبۡلُ وَلَمۡ تَكُ
شَيۡـٔٗا ٩ قَالَ رَبِّ ٱجۡعَل لِّيٓ ءَايَةٗۚ قَالَ ءَايَتُكَ أَلَّا
تُكَلِّمَ ٱلنَّاسَ ثَلَٰثَ لَيَالٖ سَوِيّٗا ١٠ فَخَرَجَ عَلَىٰ قَوۡمِهِۦ
مِنَ ٱلۡمِحۡرَابِ فَأَوۡحَىٰٓ إِلَيۡهِمۡ أَن سَبِّحُواْ بُكۡرَةٗ وَعَشِيّٗا ١١

(2–11) Zachariah عليه السلام Prays for God's Intervention

2 Here is *a reminder of your Lord's* wondrous *mercy* bestowed *upon His* venerable *servant, Zachariah.* In it are lessons for you, O Muḥammad, and for every soul that gives heed to this Book.

Behold Zachariah, *when he entreated his Lord* with devo- 3
tion *in secret entreaty,* away from the eyes of people, so
as to summon his utmost sincerity, so that the divine
answer to his prayer might come.

He was careful to observe the spiritual etiquette of 4
prayer, admitting his limitations and expressing his
thankfulness and contentment with God. *He said, "My
Lord, indeed the bones within me have weakened* with age
and the hair on *my head is lit with gray.* Your servant is
now aging. *Yet never in praying to You, my Lord*—in a
long life of devotion and worship—*have I been* left
unhappy, for You hear every sincere plea and confer
upon Your servants much favor such that all gratitude
cannot match Your care and generosity.

"My plea is worthy, O Lord, for it is burdened with 5
concern for Your religion and Your people, *and I fear
for my kinsfolk coming after me*—when my earthly life
ends. *And my wife,* also, is elderly and *is barren.* Yet You
have shown me in Your scriptures that You answered
the prayers of our forefathers—Abraham, Isaac, Jacob,
and David—when they appealed to You for righteous
children, for descendants who would be devoted to
Your religion, to setting aright the affairs of people, and
to standing against faithlessness and wrongdoing. *So
grant me* a son *from Your own bounty,* one who will be *a
successor* to me in this mission, as well as a comfort and
help to his parents in their old age.

"And cause him *to inherit from me* the mantle of prophet- 6
hood, so as to guide the Children of Israel. *And* cause

him *to inherit* the sacred knowledge of the Torah *from the Family of Jacob,* in order to lead this people in the performance of their religious rites and to bring their affairs into consonance with Your Law. *And make him, my Lord,* most of all, *well-pleasing* to You, and to the people, because of his godliness and noble character."

7 Then God called out to His servant through His angels, saying, *"O Zachariah,* hear the answer to your prayer! *Indeed, We give you glad tidings of a* blessed *boy, whose name is* to be *John. We have appointed his name to no other before,* nor granted any other before him the like of his character."

8 Zachariah received these tidings in wonderment, for he and his wife had remained childless even in the prime of life, and now they were elderly. *He said, "My Lord, how shall I have a boy, while my wife is* agéd and *barren,* unable to conceive children? *And most surely I* too *have reached an advanced old age."*

9 The angel *said* in answer to Zachariah's open wonder, *"So shall it be.* You shall have a son despite your age and despite the condition of your wife, for *your Lord has said, 'It is easy for Me* to create whomever I will. *And* recall, O Zachariah, with a comforted heart, that *most surely I have created you before, when you were nothing* at all, not yet even in existence.'" Zachariah asked God for a tangible portent that would confirm in his heart this imminent miracle.

10 *He said, "My Lord, make for me a sign* that confirms these glad tidings." God *said, "Your sign is that you shall* be

overcome with the awe of God and *not* be able to *speak to people for three straight nights* continuous, though you shall not be afflicted with any illness or impediment."

Having received the tidings of a son, Zachariah *then came* 11
forth to his people from the Sanctuary where he had been holding his prayer vigils. At once, God's sign appeared. Zachariah was unable to speak to his people—the Children of Israel. *And thus he gestured to them* that they should not emulate his silence, but that it was for them *to give glory* to God for His blessing upon them all and to recite His praises *in the morning and* in *the evening.*

يَـٰيَحۡيَىٰ خُذِ ٱلۡكِتَـٰبَ بِقُوَّةٖۖ وَءَاتَيۡنَـٰهُ ٱلۡحُكۡمَ صَبِيّٗا ﴿١٢﴾
وَحَنَانٗا مِّن لَّدُنَّا وَزَكَوٰةٗۖ وَكَانَ تَقِيّٗا ﴿١٣﴾ وَبَرَّۢا بِوَٰلِدَيۡهِ وَلَمۡ
يَكُن جَبَّارًا عَصِيّٗا ﴿١٤﴾ وَسَلَٰمٌ عَلَيۡهِ يَوۡمَ وُلِدَ وَيَوۡمَ يَمُوتُ
وَيَوۡمَ يُبۡعَثُ حَيّٗا ﴿١٥﴾

(12–15) JOHN ﷷ, THE UPHOLDER OF THE BOOK

Just as Zachariah had hoped and prayed, and as the angels had then declared, John [*Yaḥyâ*, in the Arabic of the Quran] was conceived and born to this gentle, elderly couple of patience and reverence. John's distinctiveness became evident in boyhood and manhood when he was summoned to take up his mission among the Children of Israel.

God said, *"O John,* you are a prophet, so *seize hold of the* 12
Book of God *with* all your *power* and resolve. And be not

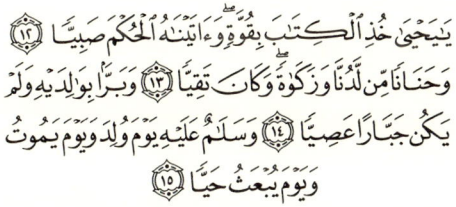

like the fainthearted among the Children of Israel who wavered and faltered in fulfilling My commandments." *And* along with revelation *We gave him wisdom,* even *as a child.*

13 *And* We gave him also *tenderness, from Our own* generosity, *and* a *purity* of soul that naturally refuses abomination; *and he was ever* and thoroughly *God-fearing,* an exemplary man.

14 *Moreover, he was* continually *virtuous to his parents,* diligent in serving them without fatigue. *And never was he insolent* to his relatives or to his people. Nor did he exploit the spiritual authority and power God clearly conferred upon him. Nor was he *disobedient* to his Lord in any matter, under any condition.

15 *So* God's *peace be upon him,* now and forevermore—and especially during the natural passages of life that carry the utmost human vulnerability: *The day he was born* into the world; *and the day he dies* when the rigors of death visit him; *and the day* when *he is raised* from the grave *to life* again—the Day of Resurrection, a terrible day for the wrongdoers!

II. The Story of Mary and the Advent of Jesus عليه السلام

As Zachariah عليه السلام had perceived, the Children of Israel had reached a watershed in their long history. Faith waned in the hearts of his people. Doubt and indulgence triumphed over sincerity in religion such that some colluded against their own prophets and breached their covenant with God. Yet God, the Ever Patient, was to give the Children of Israel an illustrious assemblage of prophets and believers, blessed with miracles so convincing that no one could be mistaken about their having come from God. Mary, from the noble Family of ʿImrân, the chosen lineage of the Children of Israel, would be the bearer of God's mercy of reform for her people.

Following upon the signs of Zachariah and upon the wondrous birth of John عليه السلام, the Children of Israel would again witness one of the most spectacular miracles of all time, the advent of the long-anticipated "anointed one," the Messiah, Jesus son of Mary. It was Jesus who was to receive a Book confirming the Torah for the Children of Israel. The revelation was to be known as the Evangel [*al-Injîl* or the Gospel]. Jesus' remarkable life begins with one of the noblest and purest women ever to touch the face of the earth.

وَٱذْكُرْ فِى ٱلْكِتَـٰبِ مَرْيَمَ إِذِ ٱنتَبَذَتْ
مِنْ أَهْلِهَا مَكَانًا شَرْقِيًّا ﴿١٦﴾ فَٱتَّخَذَتْ مِن دُونِهِمْ حِجَابًا
فَأَرْسَلْنَآ إِلَيْهَا رُوحَنَا فَتَمَثَّلَ لَهَا بَشَرًا سَوِيًّا ﴿١٧﴾ قَالَتْ إِنِّىٓ
أَعُوذُ بِٱلرَّحْمَـٰنِ مِنكَ إِن كُنتَ تَقِيًّا ﴿١٨﴾ قَالَ إِنَّمَآ أَنَا۠ رَسُولُ
رَبِّكِ لِأَهَبَ لَكِ غُلَـٰمًا زَكِيًّا ﴿١٩﴾ قَالَتْ أَنَّىٰ يَكُونُ لِى
غُلَـٰمٌ وَلَمْ يَمْسَسْنِى بَشَرٌ وَلَمْ أَكُ بَغِيًّا ﴿٢٠﴾ قَالَ كَذَٰلِكِ
قَالَ رَبُّكِ هُوَ عَلَىَّ هَيِّنٌ ۖ وَلِنَجْعَلَهُۥٓ ءَايَةً لِّلنَّاسِ وَرَحْمَةً
مِّنَّا ۚ وَكَانَ أَمْرًا مَّقْضِيًّا ﴿٢١﴾ ۞ فَحَمَلَتْهُ فَٱنتَبَذَتْ
بِهِۦ مَكَانًا قَصِيًّا ﴿٢٢﴾

(16–22) MARY'S REMARKABLE CONCEPTION OF JESUS عليه السلام ANNOUNCED THROUGH ANGEL GABRIEL عليه السلام, THE HOLY SPIRIT

16 *And mention,* O Muḥammad, to humanity all that is now being revealed to you *in the Book* of God about the wondrous story of the mother of Jesus, *Mary,* daughter of ʿImrân.[1] Tell them of *when,* in the blossom of youth, *she withdrew from her family* and retreated *to an eastern place,* to devote herself to prayer and to the remembrance of God in solitude.

17 *And she placed a veil between herself and them* to avert distraction. *Then We sent to her Our* angel-messenger whose title of honor is the Holy *Spirit,* and who is none other than the Angel Gabriel, *who thus appeared to her as a perfect human being,* so as for her not to be frightened at the sight of his true magnificent form.

When she saw him, she protested the presence of a 18
strange man in her sanctuary and feared harm from him.
She said, "Indeed, I seek refuge in the All-Merciful from you
and from any evil that may come from you. I warn you
that God punishes those who violate this holy place. So
let me be, *if ever you were God-fearing!"*

He said, "I am not a human being, nor am I an evil- 19
doer. *Indeed, I am none other than* an angel, *a messenger of*
your Lord to grant to you a pure boy. His birth shall be a
miracle and a manifest sign of his truthfulness.
Moreover, this miracle shall aid him—as a Messenger of
Resolve—to call his people back to the sincere worship
of the true God and for them to abandon the evil ways
and idol worship to which they have inclined."

Astonished by his announcement, *she said* to Angel 20
Gabriel, God's chosen Messenger of Revelation, *"How*
shall I have a baby *boy while no human being has* ever
touched me, for never have I been married, *nor have I*
ever compromised my honor and *been unchaste?"*

The angel *said,* "Even so, *thus shall it be;* you shall be 21
with child, though truly you are most innocent and virtuous; for *your Lord has said,* 'This is no difficult matter
for the Almighty; *it is easy for Me* to create whomever I
will. *And We shall* cause the child to be in you, as your
son, and thereby *make him a sign for all people* to reflect
upon and to see manifest before their eyes the might of
God. *And* he shall be a living *mercy from Us*—a human
messenger sent to the Children of Israel. *And* know, O
Mary, that *this is a matter decreed.* This is My plan, which

cannot be deterred. So do not dispute or resist it, but calm your heart and trust in your Lord.'"

So by God's leave, Angel Gabriel sent forth the breath of life into Mary's womb; and her immaculate conception of Jesus was silently established and human destiny took a new turn.

22 *So she conceived him, and withdrew with him* in-womb *to a remote place,* far from human eyes.

فَأَجَآءَهَا ٱلْمَخَاضُ إِلَىٰ جِذْعِ ٱلنَّخْلَةِ
قَالَتْ يَٰلَيْتَنِى مِتُّ قَبْلَ هَٰذَا وَكُنتُ نَسْيًا مَّنسِيًّا ﴿٢٣﴾
فَنَادَىٰهَا مِن تَحْتِهَآ أَلَّا تَحْزَنِى قَدْ جَعَلَ رَبُّكِ تَحْتَكِ سَرِيًّا ﴿٢٤﴾
وَهُزِّىٓ إِلَيْكِ بِجِذْعِ ٱلنَّخْلَةِ تُسَٰقِطْ عَلَيْكِ رُطَبًا جَنِيًّا ﴿٢٥﴾
فَكُلِى وَٱشْرَبِى وَقَرِّى عَيْنًا ۖ فَإِمَّا تَرَيِنَّ مِنَ ٱلْبَشَرِ أَحَدًا فَقُولِىٓ
إِنِّى نَذَرْتُ لِلرَّحْمَٰنِ صَوْمًا فَلَنْ أُكَلِّمَ ٱلْيَوْمَ إِنسِيًّا ﴿٢٦﴾

(23–26) Mary Gives Birth to Jesus عليه السلام Alone in a Remote Place

What worldly scale can measure God's blessing upon Mary? Yet it is a pattern in the history of righteousness that great blessings are often accompanied by immense tribulation. Young, alone, and frightened, Mary bravely sequesters herself in a grove, not only to deliver her miracle, but to strive with her soul, with life itself, in the path of God. The pain of accusation and abuse that would assault her, at the tongues of her own beloved people, can scarcely be imagined, let alone endured.

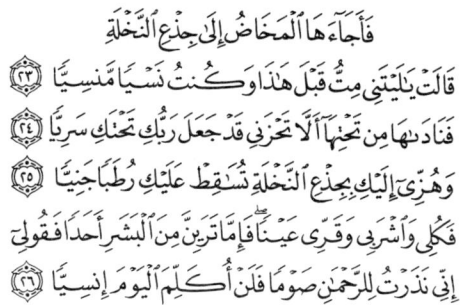

But endure she does, and God, the Giver of Security, is ever with her.

And when the blessed unborn became fully formed in her womb and his delivery was at hand, *the birth pangs drove her to the trunk of a* nearby *date-palm.* Leaning her burdened body against the tree in weariness and pain, *she said, "Oh, woe to me* for the terrible anguish and plight I now face! *If only I had died before this* day had come, *and* if only I could enter oblivion and *become something utterly forgotten* so that people would never mention me—the devotee of the Sanctuary—as one of ill fame." 23

Then a voice *called to her from beneath her*—the voice of the newborn Jesus himself—"Never fear, and *do not sorrow. Indeed, your Lord has already placed beneath you a* fresh flowing *streamlet* from which to bathe yourself and to drink.[2] 24

And shake toward you the trunk of the barren *date-palm, and it shall* flourish before your eyes and promptly *drop upon you dates, ripe and fresh.* Therein is replenishment for you, by the mercy of God, and yet another miracle, for God is always with His righteous servants. 25

So let not sorrow and grief overwhelm you; rather *eat and drink* from these blessed provisions, *and cool your eyes* for the sake of your own welfare and for the well being of your newborn. *And if you should see any human being* who inquires about your absence or protests the bundle you carry in your arms, *then* do not speak in your own defense, for God shall inspire an answer on your behalf. Simply *say, "I have vowed to* my Lord, *the All-Merciful, a* 26 *fast,* and I will not interrupt my silence. *Thus today I shall speak to no human being."*

فَأَتَتْ بِهِۦ قَوْمَهَا تَحْمِلُهُۥ ۖ قَالُوا۟ يَـٰمَرْيَمُ لَقَدْ جِئْتِ شَيْـًٔا
فَرِيًّا ﴿٢٧﴾ يَـٰٓأُخْتَ هَـٰرُونَ مَا كَانَ أَبُوكِ ٱمْرَأَ سَوْءٍ وَمَا كَانَتْ
أُمُّكِ بَغِيًّا ﴿٢٨﴾ فَأَشَارَتْ إِلَيْهِ ۖ قَالُوا۟ كَيْفَ نُكَلِّمُ مَن كَانَ فِى
ٱلْمَهْدِ صَبِيًّا ﴿٢٩﴾ قَالَ إِنِّى عَبْدُ ٱللَّهِ ءَاتَىٰنِىَ ٱلْكِتَـٰبَ وَجَعَلَنِى
نَبِيًّا ﴿٣٠﴾ وَجَعَلَنِى مُبَارَكًا أَيْنَ مَا كُنتُ وَأَوْصَـٰنِى بِٱلصَّلَوٰةِ
وَٱلزَّكَوٰةِ مَا دُمْتُ حَيًّا ﴿٣١﴾ وَبَرًّۢا بِوَٰلِدَتِى وَلَمْ يَجْعَلْنِى
جَبَّارًا شَقِيًّا ﴿٣٢﴾ وَٱلسَّلَـٰمُ عَلَىَّ يَوْمَ وُلِدتُّ وَيَوْمَ أَمُوتُ
وَيَوْمَ أُبْعَثُ حَيًّا ﴿٣٣﴾

(27–33) Mary Suffers the Chastisement of Her People to Which the Infant Jesus عليه السلام Responds

Mary returns to her household with the newborn in arm, maintaining her fast from speech. Shocked in utter disbelief at what she presents to them, her people accuse and scorn her. But in a manner nearly as spectacular as the immaculate birth, God elevates Mary and vindicates her before her family and her people on the lips of the newborn Jesus. The revelation of the Quran enshrines this moment for all time.

27 *Then she came with him to her people, carrying him*—this newborn. *They said, "O Mary!* Have you given birth to a baby though you are unwed? *Truly you have come forth with something unimaginable,* a thing that God has utterly forbidden—and you, the girl of the Sanctuary!

"O sister of Aaron,[3] who was so righteous of a man, how 28
can you, of all people, have done this depraved deed, when you are from a virtuous and God-fearing home? *Your father was not an evil person* indulged in vice, *nor was your mother* at all *unchaste* such that you could have learned such promiscuity from them!"

So having been admonished by God not to speak, *she* 29
then *pointed to* her newborn, her son Jesus, gesturing to her people, as if to say, "Ask him about the matter that now confounds you and causes you to accuse me." *They* protested such a farfetched proposition and *said, "How shall we speak to one who is in the cradle,* merely *an infant boy?* Do you take us for fools?"

> Then to the awe of all present, God, who gives all things their manner of speech, bestowed the newborn Jesus with the power to speak in his very cradle—to defend the honor of his mother, but also to declare and bear witness to a fact that would nonetheless become disputed by the ignorant, that he was indeed a messenger of God sent to the Children of Israel.

Responding to their audacious contentions, the infant 30
Jesus *said, "Indeed, I am the servant of God. He has given me the Book,* a revelation to be known as the Evangel, confirming the Torah; *and* God has chosen me from among the Children of Israel and *has made me a prophet.* I am to lead you back to worshipping Him—and Him alone—and to His covenant, the bond of honor that ennobled your fathers and all humanity.

31 *"And He has made me blessed,* as a great benefit to people, *wherever I may be; and He has enjoined upon me* the establishment and preservation of *the Prayer and* the giving of the prescribed *Charity,* each in its due time, for *as long as I am alive.*

32 *"And* I am enjoined by God *to be* gentle and *virtuous to my mother*—as are all of you; *and He has not made me* an *insolent* human being, condescending to the common people and arrogant in the land. Nor shall I make myself *wretched* with wrongdoing.

33 *"So* it is *peace* that God has ordained to *be upon me,* now and forevermore—on *the day I was born* into the world, *and the day I* am to *die, and the day* when *I am raised to life* again for judgment in the Hereafter."

ذَٰلِكَ عِيسَى ٱبْنُ مَرْيَمَ ۚ قَوْلَ ٱلْحَقِّ
ٱلَّذِى فِيهِ يَمْتَرُونَ ﴿٣٤﴾ مَا كَانَ لِلَّهِ أَن يَتَّخِذَ مِن وَلَدٍ ۖ سُبْحَٰنَهُۥٓ ۚ
إِذَا قَضَىٰٓ أَمْرًا فَإِنَّمَا يَقُولُ لَهُۥ كُن فَيَكُونُ ﴿٣٥﴾ وَإِنَّ ٱللَّهَ رَبِّى وَرَبُّكُمْ
فَٱعْبُدُوهُ ۚ هَٰذَا صِرَٰطٌ مُّسْتَقِيمٌ ﴿٣٦﴾

(34–36) God Instructs Prophet Muhammad ﷺ as to the True Nature of Jesus عليه السلام

God is He who is the Creator of everyone and everything. All submit to Him and obey His command. He has no partner in His divinity, nor agent in His creation, nor assistant to carry out His decree. If God creates someone by a command to which people are unaccustomed, in nowise does this indicate that there is divinity in such a one. Rather, it only points out that special creation took place. If such a thing were true, then all things in existence—which are God's creations and unique—would be considered the divine offspring of God. Indeed, such logic is contradicted by sincere reflection and by the teachings of all the prophets, messengers, and scriptures. Being created is altogether different from being divine, for divinity—which belongs only to God—is eternal and self-sustaining, without beginning or end, and without need, while creation is finite and dependent, no matter its condition and no matter the miracle of its creation.

He whom God has created by exceptional means becomes unique in the *manner* of his creation, not in the *matter* of his creation. This uniqueness in *manner* of creation is the case with Jesus, who has no father. A more extraordinary occurrence is that of Adam, who is without father and mother. What sets Jesus apart, then, is not an exceptional nature, which is purely human, but that God has graced him with miracles and a revealed Book as a chosen prophet-messenger. It is on this count that all who affirm the oneness of God and the fraternity of God's prophets and messengers are to revere Jesus.

Thus, Jesus is not to be worshipped, just as Adam is not to be worshipped, nor Mary, the mother of

Jesus (nor any human being or idol). Rather He who created Jesus—the one whom Jesus himself exclusively worshipped—is the one who alone is worthy of worship and all-able to answer prayers. This is none other than God Himself.

34 *That,* O Muḥammad, *is* the certain news about *Jesus, son of Mary.* It is *the* absolute *word of truth, about which they*—the People of the Book—perpetuate doubt, and over which they *bitterly contend.*

35 *It is not for God to take a son,* for He is nothing like His creatures. Nor is He a part of His own creation. And never does His creation take on something of His divine self. *Glory be to Him! When He decrees a matter*—even if it is by way of miracle—*He but says to it "Be!" and so* easily *it is!* His is a command that none can thwart.

36 Then say, O Muḥammad, as Jesus himself repeatedly said in teaching his people: *"And indeed, God is my Lord and your Lord; so worship Him* and none else. *This* is the path that I walk, and it *is a straight way,* a good path to be tread by the upright who truly love God."[4]

III. A Warning About the Coming Judgment

فَٱخْتَلَفَ ٱلْأَحْزَابُ مِنۢ
بَيْنِهِمْ ۖ فَوَيْلٌ لِّلَّذِينَ كَفَرُوا۟ مِن مَّشْهَدِ يَوْمٍ عَظِيمٍ ﴿٣٧﴾ أَسْمِعْ بِهِمْ
وَأَبْصِرْ يَوْمَ يَأْتُونَنَا ۖ لَـٰكِنِ ٱلظَّـٰلِمُونَ ٱلْيَوْمَ فِى ضَلَـٰلٍ مُّبِينٍ ﴿٣٨﴾
وَأَنذِرْهُمْ يَوْمَ ٱلْحَسْرَةِ إِذْ قُضِىَ ٱلْأَمْرُ ۚ وَهُمْ فِى غَفْلَةٍ وَهُمْ لَا يُؤْمِنُونَ
﴿٣٩﴾ إِنَّا نَحْنُ نَرِثُ ٱلْأَرْضَ وَمَنْ عَلَيْهَا وَإِلَيْنَا يُرْجَعُونَ ﴿٤٠﴾

(37–40) The Sectarian Dispute Between Christians and Jews About Jesus عليه السلام and Mary

Many people among the Jews and the Christians have taken up two extreme positions as to the person of Jesus: The former denounce him as a false Messiah, a son of illegitimate birth; the latter elevate him to the level of a god alongside God, and even God Himself. But there will come a day—a final day—in which all disputes are settled, all positions exposed, and all argumentation useless. God will call to account each one that has enrolled in this dispute, whether for denying Jesus and demeaning his honor and his mother, or for attributing godship to Jesus. But before that day, here is a scripture—the Quran—that is pure and unpolluted by the alterations of men. It says that Jesus is not God, nor is he the "son" of God. He is the Messiah, a prophet, a noble and truthful messenger from among the Messengers of Resolve.[5]

> In no manner was the birth of Jesus the result of an illicit act on the part of his mother. She was a devout woman, a virgin, and her conception of Jesus was miraculous. And may there be God's peace and blessings upon her in this life and ever after!

37 The truth of Jesus is plain, *yet the sects have disputed among themselves* about him.[6] *Woe, then, to those who disbelieve* in what has been revealed to them! Woe to them when they will recoil *from the spectacle of a great Day*—a Day of unmasked accountability! It is a Day in which every soul shall stand before God, the All-Mighty, and be asked about all that they have conjectured about God during their brief lives.

38 *How well they shall hear* the truth of this matter *and see* it for themselves *on the day they come to Us* for judgment! *But* alas *the wrongdoers* will not be helped when they realize the truth on *this day.* Rather, they *are* to see just how far they have strayed and how far they have indulged *in* what is *clear misguidance.*

39 *And warn them* all, O Muḥammad, *of* the consequences of associating false gods with the one true God, who is generous and good to people. Call them back to the worship of God exclusively, to affirm the hopeful message of His prophets, and to keep in the forefront of their minds that all men and women will die and then be given life again in the Hereafter. Tell them, so that they will set aright their faith and deeds, and that they may enjoy with their families a wholesome and success-

ful life before Judgment Day overtakes the world suddenly. Warn them that this day will be *the Day of Regret* for the wrongdoers. When the final trumpet sounds, it will be too late, *when the matter* of the ultimate destiny *is decreed, while they are* yet *heedless* of the truth and of the Hereafter, and *while they* still *do not believe* that only God is worthy of worship and that He alone receives and answers prayer.

Indeed, O people, *it is We* alone, as the Lord and Sover- 40
eign of all existence, *who shall inherit the earth* and take repossession of it *and whoever is upon it,* seen or unseen. *And to Us are they returning* for judgment.

> Thus did the blessing of prophethood reach its culmination among the family line of ʿImrân (Amram) of the Children of Israel—in Zachariah, John, and finally Jesus. The miracles that accompanied them and Mary were unmistakable signs of God's guidance. Yet long before them, God had chosen to place his message and blessing in the family line of the great forebear of prophethood, Abraham, the Friend of God.[7]

IV. Abraham عليه السلام and the Prophets of Honor

وَٱذۡكُرۡ
فِي ٱلۡكِتَٰبِ إِبۡرَٰهِيمَۚ إِنَّهُۥ كَانَ صِدِّيقٗا نَّبِيًّا ﴿٤١﴾ إِذۡ قَالَ لِأَبِيهِ يَٰٓأَبَتِ
لِمَ تَعۡبُدُ مَا لَا يَسۡمَعُ وَلَا يُبۡصِرُ وَلَا يُغۡنِي عَنكَ شَيۡـٔٗا ﴿٤٢﴾ يَٰٓأَبَتِ
إِنِّي قَدۡ جَآءَنِي مِنَ ٱلۡعِلۡمِ مَا لَمۡ يَأۡتِكَ فَٱتَّبِعۡنِيٓ أَهۡدِكَ صِرَٰطٗا
سَوِيّٗا ﴿٤٣﴾ يَٰٓأَبَتِ لَا تَعۡبُدِ ٱلشَّيۡطَٰنَۖ إِنَّ ٱلشَّيۡطَٰنَ كَانَ لِلرَّحۡمَٰنِ
عَصِيّٗا ﴿٤٤﴾ يَٰٓأَبَتِ إِنِّيٓ أَخَافُ أَن يَمَسَّكَ عَذَابٞ مِّنَ ٱلرَّحۡمَٰنِ
فَتَكُونَ لِلشَّيۡطَٰنِ وَلِيّٗا ﴿٤٥﴾ قَالَ أَرَاغِبٌ أَنتَ عَنۡ ءَالِهَتِي
يَٰٓإِبۡرَٰهِيمُۖ لَئِن لَّمۡ تَنتَهِ لَأَرۡجُمَنَّكَۖ وَٱهۡجُرۡنِي مَلِيّٗا ﴿٤٦﴾ قَالَ
سَلَٰمٌ عَلَيۡكَۖ سَأَسۡتَغۡفِرُ لَكَ رَبِّيٓۖ إِنَّهُۥ كَانَ بِي حَفِيّٗا ﴿٤٧﴾
وَأَعۡتَزِلُكُمۡ وَمَا تَدۡعُونَ مِن دُونِ ٱللَّهِ وَأَدۡعُواْ رَبِّي عَسَىٰٓ
أَلَّآ أَكُونَ بِدُعَآءِ رَبِّي شَقِيّٗا ﴿٤٨﴾ فَلَمَّا ٱعۡتَزَلَهُمۡ وَمَا يَعۡبُدُونَ
مِن دُونِ ٱللَّهِ وَهَبۡنَا لَهُۥٓ إِسۡحَٰقَ وَيَعۡقُوبَۖ وَكُلّٗا جَعَلۡنَا نَبِيّٗا ﴿٤٩﴾
وَوَهَبۡنَا لَهُم مِّن رَّحۡمَتِنَا وَجَعَلۡنَا لَهُمۡ لِسَانَ صِدۡقٍ عَلِيّٗا ﴿٥٠﴾

(41–50) The Four Appeals of Abraham عليه السلام to His Father and the Beginning of His Call

God called Abraham to establish the blessings of monotheistic faith in the world when Abraham was yet young. He was neither a Jew nor a Christian. He preceded these faith communities as the patriarch of all the prophets succeeding him. God commanded Abraham to surrender his soul to God, whereupon Abraham responded by saying, "I submit my soul to the Lord of the Worlds."

This is the basis of the covenant he passed on to his children, each a nation, Ishmael and Isaac, and to his grandson, Jacob—all of them prophets. They called this creed "the true religion"[8] and exhorted their descendants that they die only in the state of being believers of God, people who submit to His wonderful will and who accept the purposes for which He created humanity, which is the meaning of the word and name "*Muslim.*"

And mention, O Muḥammad, to humanity all that is now 41
being revealed to you *in the Book* of God about the eminent status of *Abraham.* He is the father of those prophets who descended from the lines of Ishmael and Isaac, and *indeed, he was ever-truthful,* and himself *a prophet.*

Behold the youthful Abraham when he resolved to lead 42
his family back to the worship of God. With a gentle, loving word, *he said to his father,* Âzar, in the hope of helping him to see the folly of worshipping mere stones: *"My dear father, why do you worship what can neither hear, nor see, nor avail you in anything* you hope for—unlike the power and the might of God, the Exalted?

"My dear father, indeed, sure *knowledge* from God *has come* 43
to me that has not reached you. So please *follow me* upon the path of success and accept my counsel, *and I shall guide you to an even way* upon which you shall never go astray. How happy you will be living by the guidance of your true Maker! For He will deliver you on Judgment Day from the torment of the Fire, the very destiny of those who worship false deities.

44 *"My dear father, do not worship* the evil one called *Satan,* for it is only him that you actually worship when you indulge in idolatry. And know that *indeed, Satan is ever rebellious to the All-Merciful.* Satan's mission is to mislead people by any means possible, so that they too can be rebellious against our all-loving Creator.

45 *"My dear father,* out of love and grave concern I appeal to you. For *I fear that a torment from the All-Merciful will strike you* down in punishment, if you continue in your rejection of God and in your worship of these idols. And if *such* a fate befalls you, then it shall be *that you will* forever *become a patron of Satan,* his companion not only in this life but also in the Hellfire to come."

46 Abraham's father was enraged by his son's good counsel, and his response was harsh. *He said, "Are you,* my own son, so bold as to be *averse to my gods, O Abraham,* these icons that I have fashioned with my own hands? *Most surely, if you do not desist* from your blasphemy *I will stone you* to death as a heretic. *So* be banished from this family, this people, this land, and *leave me* and my home *for a long while,* until such time as you come to your senses and repent and I may forgive you."

47 Abraham went away in exile, yet as he departed *he said* no harsh word to his father, for God enjoins kindness to parents. He offered only the farewell, *"Peace be with you.* No harm shall come to you from me." Still, his care for his father did not waver: *"I shall ask my Lord to forgive you,* that destruction may not befall you for your idolatry, for all my hope rests in God. *Indeed, He has been ever*

gracious to me, giving me true knowledge and answering my prayers.

"And I shall stay away from you and your people, as you have commanded—and stay away as well from this godless way of life *and whatever* false and powerless images *you call upon apart from God. And I shall call upon my Lord* exclusively instead, and render all my service to Him sincerely, pursuing His pleasure alone. *And* if I accomplish this, then *it may be that in calling upon my Lord* to answer my prayers *I shall not be* left *unhappy* and unfulfilled, as you surely shall be in calling upon your deaf idols." 48

So when Abraham *stayed away from them and whatever they worshipped apart from God,* and when he refused to pay homage to false gods, he fulfilled his promise. So *We granted him* a reward for his sincerity and steadfast worship of God alone, even in the face of family and societal pressure. We blessed him with a blessed son, *Isaac, and* through Isaac, a blessed grandson, *Jacob. And each one We made a prophet* after him. 49

And We granted each of *them* an abundance of blessings and grace *from Our mercy, and We set* praise *for them* upon the tongues of every succeeding generation, such that they are to this very day mentioned in high esteem and with *an exalted reverence.* 50

وَٱذْكُرْ فِى ٱلْكِتَـٰبِ مُوسَىٰٓ ۚ إِنَّهُۥ كَانَ مُخْلَصًا وَكَانَ رَسُولًا نَّبِيًّا ﴿٥١﴾
وَنَـٰدَيْنَـٰهُ مِن جَانِبِ ٱلطُّورِ ٱلْأَيْمَنِ وَقَرَّبْنَـٰهُ نَجِيًّا ﴿٥٢﴾ وَوَهَبْنَا لَهُۥ مِن
رَّحْمَتِنَآ أَخَاهُ هَـٰرُونَ نَبِيًّا ﴿٥٣﴾ وَٱذْكُرْ فِى ٱلْكِتَـٰبِ إِسْمَـٰعِيلَ ۚ إِنَّهُۥ كَانَ
صَادِقَ ٱلْوَعْدِ وَكَانَ رَسُولًا نَّبِيًّا ﴿٥٤﴾ وَكَانَ يَأْمُرُ أَهْلَهُۥ بِٱلصَّلَوٰةِ
وَٱلزَّكَوٰةِ وَكَانَ عِندَ رَبِّهِۦ مَرْضِيًّا ﴿٥٥﴾ وَٱذْكُرْ فِى ٱلْكِتَـٰبِ إِدْرِيسَ ۚ
إِنَّهُۥ كَانَ صِدِّيقًا نَّبِيًّا ﴿٥٦﴾ وَرَفَعْنَـٰهُ مَكَانًا عَلِيًّا ﴿٥٧﴾ أُو۟لَـٰٓئِكَ ٱلَّذِينَ
أَنْعَمَ ٱللَّهُ عَلَيْهِم مِّنَ ٱلنَّبِيِّـۧنَ مِن ذُرِّيَّةِ ءَادَمَ وَمِمَّنْ حَمَلْنَا مَعَ نُوحٍ
وَمِن ذُرِّيَّةِ إِبْرَٰهِيمَ وَإِسْرَٰٓءِيلَ وَمِمَّنْ هَدَيْنَا وَٱجْتَبَيْنَآ ۚ إِذَا تُتْلَىٰ عَلَيْهِمْ
ءَايَـٰتُ ٱلرَّحْمَـٰنِ خَرُّوا۟ سُجَّدًا وَبُكِيًّا ۩ ﴿٥٨﴾

(51-58) MOSES عليه السلام, AARON عليه السلام, ISHMAEL عليه السلام, AND IDRIS عليه السلام: PROPHETS OF HONORABLE MENTION

51 *And mention,* O Muḥammad, all that is now being revealed to you *in the Book* of God about the noble Prophet *Moses. Indeed, he was chosen* to deliver the Children of Israel from Pharaoh's tyranny, *and he was a messenger,* sent with the Commandments of God. And he was *a prophet* of resolve who upheld God's covenant without fail.

52 As Moses advanced toward Egypt from Midian through the Sinai, he perceived a fire on a mountain slope. *And We* Ourself *summoned him from the right side of Mount al-Ṭûr,* to impart to him the divine message and a daunting mission. *And We brought him near for close converse* in a manner conferred on no other human being.

53 God spoke to him directly from the fiery tree, commanding him to deliver his people from Egypt. *And*

when he asked God for an aide from within his own family to strengthen and assist him in conveying the message, *We granted him,* out *of Our mercy, his brother Aaron,* who was gifted in speech, and whom We appointed *as a prophet* in his own right.

And mention, O Muḥammad, to humanity all that is now 54
being revealed to you *in the Book* of God about the eldest son of Abraham, *Ishmael,* born of the blessed woman, Hagar. *Indeed, he was* the very model of a striving believer—*ever true to his promise,* never leaving his word unfulfilled, *and he* too *was a messenger.* God resettled him and his mother in the valley of Makkah to establish the blessings of the monotheistic religion among the neighboring Arabian tribes, but also to establish a city that would forever be a center of belief for all humanity. Moreover, he was *a* chosen *prophet,* favored by God to assist his father, the patriarch Abraham, in raising there the foundation of the first Sacred House of God on earth, the Kaʿba—a station to remind humanity of the truth of God and His messengers until the end of time.

Ishmael *used to* steadfastly *enjoin his family with the Prayer* 55
and with the giving of prescribed *Charity* to the needy. He exhorted them to do righteous deeds that were pleasing to God, *and he* himself *was to his Lord ever-pleasing.*

And mention, O Muḥammad, *in the Book* about the 56
learned believer *Idrīs.*[9] *Indeed, he was ever-truthful* to God, to himself, and to all people. And he was of great faith and wisdom. He too was *a prophet,* who conveyed God's message to his people.

57 *And* thus *We raised him to* an elevated rank in this life, and to *a high place* in the Hereafter.

58 *These are the ones* whom God has promoted to the true leadership of humanity. What great exemplars of excellent character and faith! Their stories and righteous ways are related to you in this Quran, for it is *upon* the likes of these *whom God* has *bestowed grace—from the prophets of the children of Adam; and from those* believers *whom We carried with Noah* in the Ark; *and from the children of Abraham and* his grandson Jacob, known also as *Israel; and from those* men and women who strove in the path of God, they *whom We guided and selected* as witnesses to the truth.

So genuine was their sincerity and so deep their faith that *when the verses of the All-Merciful were recited to them*—revealing to them sacred knowledge of the rites of worship which they were to perform and the laws by which they were to abide in life—*they fell to the ground, bowing down and weeping,* out of supreme gratitude, reverence, and love for God.

فَخَلَفَ مِنۢ بَعۡدِهِمۡ
خَلۡفٌ أَضَاعُواْ ٱلصَّلَوٰةَ وَٱتَّبَعُواْ ٱلشَّهَوَٰتِۖ فَسَوۡفَ يَلۡقَوۡنَ غَيًّا
﴿٥٩﴾ إِلَّا مَن تَابَ وَءَامَنَ وَعَمِلَ صَٰلِحٗا فَأُوْلَٰٓئِكَ يَدۡخُلُونَ ٱلۡجَنَّةَ
وَلَا يُظۡلَمُونَ شَيۡـٔٗا ﴿٦٠﴾ جَنَّٰتِ عَدۡنٍ ٱلَّتِي وَعَدَ ٱلرَّحۡمَٰنُ عِبَادَهُۥ
بِٱلۡغَيۡبِۚ إِنَّهُۥ كَانَ وَعۡدُهُۥ مَأۡتِيّٗا ﴿٦١﴾ لَّا يَسۡمَعُونَ فِيهَا لَغۡوًا إِلَّا سَلَٰمٗاۖ
وَلَهُمۡ رِزۡقُهُمۡ فِيهَا بُكۡرَةٗ وَعَشِيّٗا ﴿٦٢﴾ تِلۡكَ ٱلۡجَنَّةُ ٱلَّتِي نُورِثُ مِنۡ
عِبَادِنَا مَن كَانَ تَقِيّٗا ﴿٦٣﴾

(59–63) The Struggle of Good over Evil Among the Descendants of Abraham عليه السلام

Then descending from them thereafter, from their very seed, 59
came godless peoples, *descendants who* started upon a dark path and who eventually *forsook the Prayer.* They dishonored and neglected the prescribed rites of worship that illuminate the human soul. *And* they *followed* instead their *whims* and lusts. *And thus shall they meet with degradation* as a consequence of their sedition.

They shall endure chastisement, as they have been 60
warned—*except* for *those* among them *who* realize their error, *repent* of their unbelief, *and believe* ever after in God with genuine devotion. *And* provided they *do righteous deeds* that confirm their true repentance, God will accept it of them. Then *they shall enter the* eternal *Garden,* amply rewarded for their renewed faith and good works. Happy, then, is their meeting with God in the Hereafter, *and they shall not be wronged in anything.*

Therein do they partake of the everlasting delights 61

reserved only for those in the *Gardens of Eden.* That is the ecstasy *which the All-Merciful has promised His servants* who remain constant in their earthly lives, certain of the Hereafter, though its manifestation is kept hidden from them *in the unseen. Indeed, His promise* to His faithful worshippers *ever comes true.*

62 In Heaven, they know only gladness forever—families and friends living together in endless peace, enraptured in their nearness to God. *They shall not hear therein idle talk,* words of folly, malice, and envy; *but only* the word of *"Peace"*—a salutation to them from their Lord on high, and His angels. *And for them therein shall be their* sumptuous *provision*—food and pure drink, gems and silk clothing; fruit from every orchard and rivers gently flowing; gardens full and lush and tall trees lightly swaying; fair companions and seats of honor and fountains ever cascading—and all that enchants the heart, *morning and evening.*

63 *This is* but a glimpse of *the Garden,* the true and only Heaven, *which We shall give as inheritance to those of Our servants who are God-fearing,* those who choose purity over defilement, and who do what is right, no matter the earthly consequence.

V. Angelic Assurance and Human Doubt

وَمَا نَتَنَزَّلُ إِلَّا بِأَمْرِ رَبِّكَ لَهُۥ مَا بَيْنَ
أَيْدِينَا وَمَا خَلْفَنَا وَمَا بَيْنَ ذَٰلِكَ وَمَا كَانَ رَبُّكَ نَسِيًّا ﴿٦٤﴾
رَّبُّ ٱلسَّمَٰوَٰتِ وَٱلْأَرْضِ وَمَا بَيْنَهُمَا فَٱعْبُدْهُ وَٱصْطَبِرْ لِعِبَٰدَتِهِۦ
هَلْ تَعْلَمُ لَهُۥ سَمِيًّا ﴿٦٥﴾

(64–65) THE ANGELS AND THEIR WITNESS TO HUMANITY THAT GOD IS THE SOLE AND UNIVERSAL SOVEREIGN

> Human beings perceive very little of all that God has created. Yet God opens the senses of His prophets to apprehend something of His creation's vast unseen realities. Among the most magnificent of God's creatures are the angels, created of pure light. Unfailing in their worship and service to God, the angels carry out God's bidding between heaven and earth, record the deeds of His creatures, and inspire goodness and right action in believers. The prophets are given the honor of interacting with the angels. Chief among these angelic ranks is the Angel Gabriel عليه السلام. He is the one who has conveyed God's revelations to the prophets, including that of the Quran to the Prophet Muḥammad ﷺ.

Gabriel says to you, O Muḥammad, as part of this 64
Quran, *"And we* angels *do not descend* from the heavens

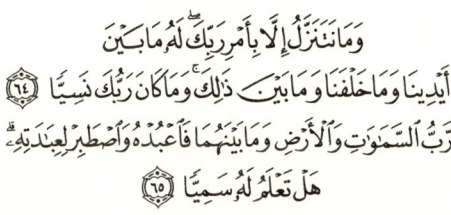

but at the command of your Lord. To Him, and to Him alone, *belongs what is* manifest and the mysteries of new events and creations that lie *before us,* including that which is to come after our deaths. *And* He alone knows *what* there *is* of creation and of eternity that lie *behind us,* deeds already done, even prior to our existence. *And* only He has power over *what* time *is* left *between this* term of life and the Day of Judgment. Thus does God encompass all things in His knowledge. *And never is your Lord forgetful* of anything!

65 He is the unchallenged Master and *Lord of the heavens and the earth and* Lord of *what is between them. So worship Him* alone, O Muḥammad, and do not take any other as a god alongside Him. *And have patience,* and persevere *in His worship*—you and whoever embraces, with full heart, the divine guidance that is revealed to you. *Do you know any other who* can bear His holy name or who possesses even a shade *of any semblance to Him!* Not a thing that has ever been or that shall be—no single creature or a combination thereof—compares with His divine reality, attributes, or acts."

وَيَقُولُ ٱلْإِنسَٰنُ أَءِذَا مَا مِتُّ لَسَوْفَ
أُخْرَجُ حَيًّا ﴿٦٦﴾ أَوَلَا يَذْكُرُ ٱلْإِنسَٰنُ أَنَّا خَلَقْنَٰهُ مِن قَبْلُ
وَلَمْ يَكُ شَيْـًٔا ﴿٦٧﴾ فَوَرَبِّكَ لَنَحْشُرَنَّهُمْ وَٱلشَّيَٰطِينَ ثُمَّ
لَنُحْضِرَنَّهُمْ حَوْلَ جَهَنَّمَ جِثِيًّا ﴿٦٨﴾ ثُمَّ لَنَنزِعَنَّ مِن كُلِّ
شِيعَةٍ أَيُّهُمْ أَشَدُّ عَلَى ٱلرَّحْمَٰنِ عِتِيًّا ﴿٦٩﴾ ثُمَّ لَنَحْنُ أَعْلَمُ بِٱلَّذِينَ
هُمْ أَوْلَىٰ بِهَا صِلِيًّا ﴿٧٠﴾ وَإِن مِّنكُمْ إِلَّا وَارِدُهَا كَانَ عَلَىٰ رَبِّكَ
حَتْمًا مَّقْضِيًّا ﴿٧١﴾ ثُمَّ نُنَجِّى ٱلَّذِينَ ٱتَّقَوا۟ وَّنَذَرُ ٱلظَّٰلِمِينَ
فِيهَا جِثِيًّا ﴿٧٢﴾

(66–72) The Ultimate Destiny of Arrogance

God has spread countless and various signs of His existence throughout the heavens and the earth and within our own souls. Some of these portents—like the miraculous story of Mary and the birth of Jesus, or like the speech of God to Moses—have been truly wondrous. Others, such as the celestial bodies, the ships plowing the seas, and the event of life itself, are no less marvelous. They require only conscious reflection upon their exquisite beauty—as well as their uncanny coherence within existence—to rouse within our souls the remembrance of God, our Maker and Judge. Furthermore, God has revealed scriptures that have made plain to people in their own languages the truth of His divine oneness. These revelations were conveyed to them by men who exemplified the godly life that these people were to live. Yet despite the abundant evidence arrayed before the human intellect and imprinted upon the soul, there are those who deny God or who insist on believing in Him only when they attribute to Him fictions that they themselves concoct.

66 Upon being told that God shall surely and easily resurrect humanity for judgment, an arrogant *man says* in disbelief, *"Can it be that when I have died* and am decomposed that *I shall be brought forth* from the earth whole again and *alive?* What absurdity!"[10]

67 *Does man not remember that We indeed created him before, and he was* once *nothing* at all in existence?

68 *Then* teach people, O Muḥammad, that *by your Lord, We shall most surely* resurrect all people, including those who deny God and those who reject the Hereafter. And We shall *round them up* all together—*as well as* those unseen creatures of evil, *the satans,* whom they have befriended. *Then most surely We shall bring them* gruffly *around Hell,* and such terror shall grip their hearts that no haughty soul will be able to stand upright on that Day. The evildoers all shall buckle and find themselves *on* their *knees.*

69 *Then We shall pluck from every* cowering *cluster* of disbelievers gathered around Hell *whichever of them was most intense in defying* and disobeying *the All-Merciful* and throw them first into it headlong.

70 *Then* know that *We, indeed, are most knowing about those who are most deserving of* entering its inferno and *roasting in it.*

And there is not one of you, O people, *but will come to* 71
Hellfire to see with your own eyes that what God has
promised in His revelations is utterly true. You shall be
compelled to cross over *it* upon the Traverse [called
Ṣirâṭ], which God will lay down between the Plain of
Judgment and Paradise. This is decided, for *it is, with
your Lord, an inevitability decreed* from all eternity.

Then We shall deliver to Paradise *those who have been God-* 72
fearing and heedful of their Lord, who strove to live by
His guidance. *And* as the pious cross over into the
Garden, *We shall leave the wrongdoers* to the tongues of
the Fire—alone *in it, on* their *knees,* to suffer for their
obstinate rejection of faith though many teachers came
to warn them and deliver them.

وَإِذَا تُتْلَىٰ عَلَيْهِمْ ءَايَٰتُنَا بَيِّنَٰتٍ قَالَ ٱلَّذِينَ كَفَرُوا۟
لِلَّذِينَ ءَامَنُوٓا۟ أَىُّ ٱلْفَرِيقَيْنِ خَيْرٌ مَّقَامًا وَأَحْسَنُ نَدِيًّا ﴿٧٣﴾ وَكَمْ
أَهْلَكْنَا قَبْلَهُم مِّن قَرْنٍ هُمْ أَحْسَنُ أَثَٰثًا وَرِءْيًا ﴿٧٤﴾ قُلْ مَن
كَانَ فِى ٱلضَّلَٰلَةِ فَلْيَمْدُدْ لَهُ ٱلرَّحْمَٰنُ مَدًّا ۚ حَتَّىٰٓ إِذَا رَأَوْا۟ مَا يُوعَدُونَ
إِمَّا ٱلْعَذَابَ وَإِمَّا ٱلسَّاعَةَ فَسَيَعْلَمُونَ مَنْ هُوَ شَرٌّ مَّكَانًا
وَأَضْعَفُ جُندًا ﴿٧٥﴾ وَيَزِيدُ ٱللَّهُ ٱلَّذِينَ ٱهْتَدَوْا۟ هُدًى ۗ
وَٱلْبَٰقِيَٰتُ ٱلصَّٰلِحَٰتُ خَيْرٌ عِندَ رَبِّكَ ثَوَابًا وَخَيْرٌ مَّرَدًّا ﴿٧٦﴾

(73–76) The Gift of Increase in What One Desires in This World

Those who choose to reject faith in the one true God and in His messengers offer nothing in evidence of their choice but whim and speculation. Yet when they are confronted with the revealed word of God as proof that God is ever-living and that the Hereafter is coming, their only rebuttal is to contemptuously label those who believe as weak-minded or extremists, and they demean their social standing. The deniers themselves desire only the fleeting life of this world, and God indeed extends it to them. But the believers long for God, so He guides them to goodness and to His loving kindness and to the everlasting bliss of an enchanted and wonderfully pleasing Afterlife.

73 God states: *When Our clear verses* from the Quran *are recited to them,* affirming that there is no deity but God, that Muḥammad is His messenger, and that Judgment

Day is drawing near, *those who disbelieve* feebly dispute the truth with bigotry. They *say to those who believe, "Which of the two groups,* ours or yours, *is of a better station* in this world? Who has more power and wealth? *And* which of us is of the *fairer company,* the more admired among people?"

What delusions do the arrogant contrive for themselves? 74
Have they not learned history's most awesome lesson? *And how many a generation before them have We destroyed* after they grew enamored with their own handiwork and accomplishments, swelled up with pride, then disbelieved in God and spread their corruption in the land? *They were* nations *of* far *fairer furnishing and* finer *appearance* than are these who have come after them impudently denying the truth of their ultimate return to God.

Say to the disbelievers, O Muḥammad: *"Whichever* of us 75
is mired *in* the delusion of *the stray way,* and resists the guidance that has come from heaven, *may the All-Merciful* God *extend the duration* of oblivion *for them! And at last, when suddenly they see* with their own eyes *what they have been promised—whether* it is *the torment* of this life that whelms the wicked *or the* abrupt coming of *the Hour* of Judgment—*then they shall know* well *who* in reality *is lowest in position and weakest in force."* And such is God's way with those who stubbornly disbelieve in Him.

Yet God ever *increases those who are* readily *guided* by His 76
religion *with* more *guidance,* and this renews them throughout their lives. *And the abiding deeds of righteousness are better* compensated in the Hereafter *with your*

Lord, for these deeds earn one eternal joy *in reward and* are *better* for the believers, *in* their ultimate *return* to God. They are better than the fleeting things of this world, in which those who deny God so love to revel.

VI. God Is One, the Source of Pure Love

أَفَرَءَيْتَ ٱلَّذِى كَفَرَ بِـَٔايَـٰتِنَا وَقَالَ لَأُوتَيَنَّ مَالًا وَوَلَدًا
﴿٧٧﴾ أَطَّلَعَ ٱلْغَيْبَ أَمِ ٱتَّخَذَ عِندَ ٱلرَّحْمَـٰنِ عَهْدًا ﴿٧٨﴾ كَلَّا ۚ
سَنَكْتُبُ مَا يَقُولُ وَنَمُدُّ لَهُۥ مِنَ ٱلْعَذَابِ مَدًّا ﴿٧٩﴾ وَنَرِثُهُۥ
مَا يَقُولُ وَيَأْتِينَا فَرْدًا ﴿٨٠﴾

(77–80) The Folly of the Disbeliever Who Thinks That Fortune and Fair Company Await Him in the Hereafter

77 *Then have you seen,* O Muḥammad, *him who* has taken idols for worship and *disbelieved in Our signs and* then *said* in boast: *"I shall surely be given wealth and children* in the Hereafter, the likes of what I have been given in this life—or more!"?

78 *Has* this insolent one *looked into the Unseen* and learned with certainty what awaits him in the Hereafter? *Or has he taken with the All-Merciful a* solemn *covenant* guaranteeing what God will give to him in eternity?

79 *No, indeed!* He lies! *We shall certainly write down* in Our ledger *what he says*—as well as every falsehood he has forged against God. *And We shall extend for him the dura-*

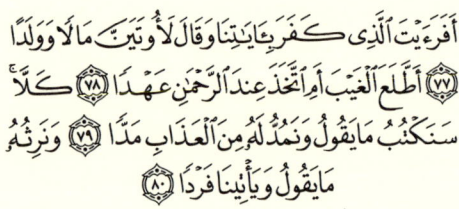

tion of the torment that most assuredly awaits him in the Hereafter.

And it is *We* alone who *shall inherit from him* in the 80
Hereafter *what* children and wealth *he* so pompously *speaks of*—for none but the godly shall have their blessings therein. *And* as for the likes of him, *he shall come to Us alone,* utterly bereft of any property, progeny, helper, or wealth that could deliver him.

وَٱتَّخَذُوا۟ مِن دُونِ ٱللَّهِ ءَالِهَةً
لِّيَكُونُوا۟ لَهُمْ عِزًّا ﴿٨١﴾ كَلَّا ۚ سَيَكْفُرُونَ بِعِبَادَتِهِمْ وَيَكُونُونَ
عَلَيْهِمْ ضِدًّا ﴿٨٢﴾ أَلَمْ تَرَ أَنَّآ أَرْسَلْنَا ٱلشَّيَٰطِينَ عَلَى ٱلْكَٰفِرِينَ
تَؤُزُّهُمْ أَزًّا ﴿٨٣﴾ فَلَا تَعْجَلْ عَلَيْهِمْ ۖ إِنَّمَا نَعُدُّ لَهُمْ عَدًّا ﴿٨٤﴾
يَوْمَ نَحْشُرُ ٱلْمُتَّقِينَ إِلَى ٱلرَّحْمَٰنِ وَفْدًا ﴿٨٥﴾ وَنَسُوقُ ٱلْمُجْرِمِينَ
إِلَىٰ جَهَنَّمَ وِرْدًا ﴿٨٦﴾ لَّا يَمْلِكُونَ ٱلشَّفَٰعَةَ إِلَّا مَنِ ٱتَّخَذَ عِندَ
ٱلرَّحْمَٰنِ عَهْدًا ﴿٨٧﴾

(81–87) In the Hereafter, All False Gods Will Disavow Those Who Used to Worship Them

Whoever mingles the worship of God with other beings 81
has gone far astray, *and* that is because *they have taken* false *gods* to pray to and adore *apart from God.* They venerate idols hoping *that* these false deities *may* intercede with God and *be for them a* means to *power* and protection.

No, indeed! God has given no share of His divinity to 82
any other. Thus on the Day of Judgment, God shall confer the power of speech upon these idols. And *they*

shall explicitly *deny* those who worshipped them and shall at once disavow *their worship; and the idolaters* in turn *will* belie their idols and repudiate their divinity. *And* right then and there *they shall be as* terrible *opponents to one another,* each party desperately negating what the other has claimed.

83 *Have you not seen,* O Muḥammad, *that* even in the life of this world *We have sent the satans against the disbelievers* as punishment for their rejection of God? So the evil ones disperse amongst them *to instigate them* to thoughts and deeds that bring them and their societies to misery. Thus some disbelievers are lured into deviance *with a vehement* effort of *instigation* that draws them away from the straight path.

84 *So make no haste concerning them,* for the ultimate end of the disbelievers shall surely come. *We but number for them a determined number* of days and catalogue their deeds on earth—and not a single thing they do escapes Our knowledge.

85 There shall come *the Day* of Resurrection when at last *We assemble the God-fearing* in a magnificent pageant of reward; *before the All-Merciful* they shall stand *in honored delegations,* for they were unfailing in belief, righteous in deed, and repentant.

86 *And* there—parch-throated, bedraggled, rounded up like cattle—also stand the brethren in evil. These are the disbelievers, the idolaters, those who associated false gods with God, and the satans. *We* shall *drive the trespassers to Hell in droves.*

Indeed, *none holds the* right of *intercession,* either for one- 87
self or for another, *but those who have* been promised this privilege and *taken with the All-Merciful a* sacred *covenant* beforehand, such as the prophets and the angels. Only their address has the All-Holy permitted on the Day of Judgment.

وَقَالُوا اتَّخَذَ الرَّحْمَٰنُ وَلَدًا ﴿٨٨﴾ لَّقَدْ
جِئْتُمْ شَيْئًا إِدًّا ﴿٨٩﴾ تَكَادُ السَّمَاوَاتُ يَتَفَطَّرْنَ مِنْهُ
وَتَنشَقُّ الْأَرْضُ وَتَخِرُّ الْجِبَالُ هَدًّا ﴿٩٠﴾ أَن دَعَوْا لِلرَّحْمَٰنِ وَلَدًا
﴿٩١﴾ وَمَا يَنبَغِي لِلرَّحْمَٰنِ أَن يَتَّخِذَ وَلَدًا ﴿٩٢﴾ إِن كُلُّ مَن فِي
السَّمَاوَاتِ وَالْأَرْضِ إِلَّا آتِي الرَّحْمَٰنِ عَبْدًا ﴿٩٣﴾ لَّقَدْ أَحْصَاهُمْ
وَعَدَّهُمْ عَدًّا ﴿٩٤﴾ وَكُلُّهُمْ آتِيهِ يَوْمَ الْقِيَامَةِ فَرْدًا ﴿٩٥﴾

(88–95) The Blasphemy of Ascribing a Child to God

There is no deity other than God. He alone creates, and He is exalted above all that He has created. The heavens and the earth, and every kind and part of creation, are immanently aware of this truth. It is only the deluded who pervert their souls' original purity by making false claims about God and engaging in continual sin.

And among humanity, there are some who profess 88
belief in God, but attribute to him a most heinous lie. *They have said, "The All-Merciful has taken a son,"* or that the angels are His daughters and the jinn His offspring.

89 *Truly you have come forth with something* utterly base and *abominable.*

90 *From it the heavens nearly burst* with indignity, *and the earth* all but *splits* in outrage, *and the mountains* nearly *fall down, collapsing* in angry protest,

91 *that they*—creatures whom God has given the gift of intellect as a favored creation—*should* ignorantly and presumptuously *ascribe to the All-Merciful a son,*

92 *while* clearly *it is not befitting to the All-Merciful*—the perfect Creator of all things—*that He* should *take a son.* He is the Self-Sufficient, in need of no one and nothing. His relationship with His creation is that of Lord and Master. He bestows life, sustains it at every moment, and gives provision. He imparts death and raises the dead. He is the Almighty. He is the One, indivisible eternally.

93 *Indeed, every* single *being in the heavens and the earth*—every angel, every human—*but comes to the All-Merciful as a servant,* a subject of the true King. And on the Day of Judgment, there is not a solitary creature but that it shall declare that God *is* God, the sole Creator, that He alone is worthy of worship.

94 *Truly, He has enumerated them* all, knowing exactly how many of His creatures there are and how each one fares, *and He has numbered them with a precise number.* Not one of them shall slip away from his or her ultimate destiny.

95 *And each one of them is coming to Him on the Day of Resurrection alone;* and there shall be none to aid anoth-

er but God. Nothing but sincere belief, righteous deeds, and a sound heart shall be of benefit.

إِنَّ ٱلَّذِينَ ءَامَنُوا۟ وَعَمِلُوا۟ ٱلصَّٰلِحَٰتِ سَيَجْعَلُ لَهُمُ
ٱلرَّحْمَٰنُ وُدًّا ﴿٩٦﴾ فَإِنَّمَا يَسَّرْنَٰهُ بِلِسَانِكَ لِتُبَشِّرَ بِهِ
ٱلْمُتَّقِينَ وَتُنذِرَ بِهِۦ قَوْمًا لُّدًّا ﴿٩٧﴾ وَكَمْ أَهْلَكْنَا قَبْلَهُم
مِّن قَرْنٍ هَلْ تُحِسُّ مِنْهُم مِّنْ أَحَدٍ أَوْ تَسْمَعُ لَهُمْ رِكْزًۢا ﴿٩٨﴾

(96–98) God's Promise of Love for His True-Hearted Servants

As for those who believe and do righteous deeds, they adhere 96
to God's revealed guidance and cleave to the original state of their pure human nature—which inclines not to sin but to good. *For them, the All-Merciful ordains pure love* in their hearts. They shall know such love among themselves in this life. The angels shall show them love on the Day of Judgment. And God shall draw them near to Him with kindness eternally, for He indeed is the All-Gracious, the All-Loving.

Thus We have indeed made this Quran of pristine Arabic, 97
O Muḥammad, that *it* may flow *easy in your* native *tongue,* endure for humanity in its original language, and yield its revealed wisdom to remembrance and understanding for the benefit of all humanity. *For* it is *you,* and your community, who are *to give glad tidings with* this Quran *to the God-fearing* of all nations that God lives and never dies and that Paradise awaits the faithful. *And*

you are *to warn therewith* every ear deaf to God's word of truth and every eye turned blind to His clear signs that Hellfire hungers for those who deny God's divinity and oneness. Those who refuse to repent—who grow belligerent against those who call them to faith—they are the advocates of corruption and falsehood on earth; and they are indeed *a* severely *contentious people.*

Accordingly, O Prophet, feel no sorrow if your people turn away from justice and falsely charge you, for God is well able to seize them from where they least suspect. That is the recompense for the lies that they utter and for the evil they have done. Rather, there is hope for the believer of every prophet's call that God is one.

98 *And how many a generation* that has utterly perished from the face of the earth *have We* already *destroyed before them.* They were a people who lived before those who now receive this call! They once grew arrogant in the land and proud of their grand achievements; and they resisted the truth and wronged their own souls. But then their day was done. *Do you perceive even one of them, or hear from them a single sound?*

COMMENTARY NOTES

1. For a full discussion on ʿImrân and the possible implications of this epithet, see the following Appendix, "'Daughter of ʿImrân' and "Sister of Aaron.'"

2. The voice, commentators say, alternatively may have been that of an angel or of the trunk of the date-palm, against which she leaned.

3. This may be an allusion to Mary being a descendant of Aaron, the brother of Moses. Or she may have had a sibling named Aaron who was renowned for his righteousness. (See the Appendix, *Daughter of* ᶜ*Imrân*).

4. Some scholars believe that the speaker here is Jesus عليه السلام, representing what he had preached to his people, while other scholars believe the words to be put by God into the mouth of Prophet Muḥammad ﷺ, reinforcing what all the prophets had said.

5. "The Messengers of Resolve" is a title given to five prophets: Noah عليه السلام, Abraham عليه السلام, Moses عليه السلام, Jesus عليه السلام, and Muḥammad ﷺ.

6. In light of the Quran's revelation of the dispute among the People of the Book, it is interesting to read Bart D. Ehrman's observation of early Christian history and the various positions and beliefs taken with regard to Jesus عليه السلام. See *The Orthodox Corruption of Scripture: The Effect of Early Christological Controversies on the Text of the New Testament* (Oxford: Oxford University Press, 1993), p. 3.

   > Christianity in the second and third centuries was in a remarkable state of flux. . . . Nowhere is this seen more clearly than in the realm of theology. In the second and third centuries there were, of course, Christians who believed in only one God; others, however, claimed that there were two Gods; yet others subscribed to 30, or 365, or more. Some Christians accepted the Hebrew Scriptures as a revelation of the one true God, the sacred possession of all believers; others claimed that the Scriptures had been inspired by an evil deity. Some Christians believed that God had created the world and was soon going to redeem it; others said that God neither had created the world nor had ever had any dealings with it. Some Christians believed that Christ was somehow both a man and God; others said that he was a man, but not God; others claimed that he was God, but not a man; others insisted that he was a man who had been temporarily inhabited by God. Some Christians believed that Christ's death had brought about the salvation of the world; others claimed that his death had no bearing on salvation; yet others alleged that he had never even died.

7. Quran, 4:125.

8. The Quran states: *And who shall be averse to the ways of Abraham, except those who are themselves fool-minded. And We have truly chosen him in this world—and in the Hereafter he shall surely be of the righteous. When his Lord said to him, "submit yourself," he said, "I submit myself to the Lord of the Worlds." And Abraham enjoined his children with this, as did Jacob: "O my children, indeed God has chosen for you the ˹true˺ religion. Therefore do not die ˹any of you˺ without ensuring that you are Muslims [that is, of those who submit their will wholly to the will of God]." Or were you witnesses when death approached Jacob, when he said to his children: "What will you worship after me?" They said, "We worship your God and the God of your forefathers, Abraham and Ishmael and Isaac. He is one God, and to Him we submit."* (Quran, 2:130–33)

9. The Prophet Idrîs ﷺ may be the prophet referred to as Enoch.

10. There are various reports that this verse refers to one (or more) of the leading disbelievers of the Quraysh in Makkah who opposed the Prophet ﷺ, such as al-ᶜÂṣ ibn Wâ'il, ᶜUbay ibn Khalaf, Abû Jahl, or al-Walîd ibn al-Mughîrah.

INTERPRETATION

English Interpretation of Sûrat Maryam

In the name of God, the All-Merciful, the Mercy-Giving.

1 *Kâf Hâ Yâ ʿAyn Ṣâd*
2 A reminder of your Lord's mercy
upon His servant Zachariah,
3 when he entreated his Lord
in secret entreaty.
4 He said, "My Lord,
indeed the bones within me
have weakened and my head is lit
with gray. Yet never
in praying to You,
my Lord, have I been unhappy.
5 And I fear for my kinsfolk
coming after me, and my wife is
barren. So grant me, from Your
own bounty, a successor

6 to inherit from me and to inherit
from the Family of Jacob;
and make him, my Lord,
well-pleasing."
7 ˹God said,˺ "O Zachariah,
Indeed, We give you glad tidings
of a boy, whose name is *John*.
We have appointed his name
to no other before."
8 He said, "My Lord,
how shall I have a boy,
while my wife is barren
and most surely I have reached
an advanced old age?"
9 ˹It was˺ said, "So shall it be!
Your Lord has said,
'It is easy for Me, and most surely I
have created you before
when you were nothing.'"
10 He said, "My Lord,
make for me a sign."
He said, "Your sign is that
you shall not ˹be able to˺ speak to
people for three straight nights."
11 Then ˹Zachariah˺ came forth to his
people from the Sanctuary,
and thus he gestured to them
to give glory in the morning
and the evening.
12 ˹God said,˺ "O John,
seize hold of the Book with power."
And We gave him wisdom
as a child,

13 and tenderness, from Our own,
and purity; and he was
ever God-fearing.
14 Moreover, he was virtuous to his
parents, and never was he insolent,
disobedient.
15 So peace be upon him
the day he was born,
and the day he dies,
and the day he is raised to life.

16 And mention in the Book
Mary, when she withdrew from her
family to an eastern place,
17 and she placed a veil between herself
and them. Then We sent to her Our
Spirit, who thus appeared to her
as a perfect human being.
18 She said, "Indeed, I seek refuge in
˹God˺ the All-Merciful from you,
if ever you were God-fearing!"
19 He said, "Indeed, I am none other
than a messenger of your Lord
to grant to you
a pure boy."
20 She said, "How shall I have a boy
while no human being
has ever touched me,
nor have I ever been unchaste?"
21 He said, "Thus shall it be!
Your Lord has said,
'It is easy for Me.
And We shall make him

a sign for all people, and a mercy
from Us—and it is
a matter decreed.'"
22 So she conceived him
and withdrew with him
to a remote place.
23 And the birth pangs drove her
to the trunk of a date-palm.
She said, "Oh, woe to me! If only I
had died before this and become
something utterly forgotten!"
24 Then he ˹who was delivered˺ called
to her from beneath her, "Do not
sorrow. Indeed, your Lord has
already placed beneath you
a streamlet.
25 And shake toward you the trunk of
the date-palm, and it shall drop upon
you dates, ripe and fresh.
26 So eat and drink and cool your eyes.
And if you should see any human
being, then say, 'I have vowed to
the All-Merciful a fast. Thus today I
shall speak to no human being.'"
27 Then she came with him
to her people, carrying him.
They said, "O Mary!
Truly you have come forth with
something unimaginable!
28 O sister of Aaron, your father was
not an evil person, nor was your
mother unchaste."
29 So ˹Mary˺ pointed to ˹the newborn˺.

They said, "How shall we speak
to one who is in the cradle,
an infant boy?"
30 ˹Baby Jesus˺ said, "Indeed,
I am the servant of God.
He has given me the Book
and He has made me a prophet.
31 And He has made me blessed
wherever I may be; and He has
enjoined upon me the Prayer and
Charity, as long as I am alive,
32 and being virtuous to my mother;
and He has not made me
insolent, wretched.
33 So peace be upon me
the day I was born,
and the day I die,
and the day I am raised to life."

34 That is Jesus, son of Mary,
the word of truth, about whom
they bitterly contend.
35 It is not for God to take a son.
Glory be to Him!
When He decrees a matter,
He but says to it "Be!" and so it is.
36 ˹Say, O Muḥammad,˺ "And indeed,
God is my Lord and your Lord;
so worship Him.
This is a straight way."

37 Yet the sects have disputed among
themselves. Then woe to those who

disbelieve—from the spectacle
of a great Day!
38 How well they shall hear and see on
the day they come to Us!
But the wrongdoers this day
are in clear misguidance.
39 And warn them of
the Day of Regret when
the matter is decreed,
while they are heedless,
while they do not believe.
40 Indeed, it is We who shall inherit
the earth and whoever is upon it,
and to Us are they returning.

41 And mention in the Book
Abraham. Indeed, he was ever-
truthful, a prophet.
42 Behold, he said to his father,
"My dear father,
why do you worship what can
neither hear, nor see,
nor avail you in anything?
43 My dear father,
indeed, knowledge has come to me
that has not reached you. So follow
me, and I shall guide you
to an even way.
44 My dear father,
do not worship Satan. Indeed, Satan
is ever rebellious to the All-Merciful.
45 My dear father,
I fear that a torment from ˹God˺

the All-Merciful will strike you;
thus you will become
a patron of Satan."
46 He said, "Are you averse to my
gods, O Abraham? Most surely,
if you do not desist, I will stone you.
So leave me for a long while."
47 ˹Abraham˺ said, "Peace be with you!
I shall ask my Lord to forgive you.
Indeed, He has been ever gracious
to me.
48 And I shall stay away from you and
whatever you call upon ˹in worhsip˺
apart from God. And I shall call upon
my Lord. And it may be that in calling
upon my Lord I shall not be unhappy."
49 So when he stayed away from them
and whatever they worshipped apart
from God, We granted him Isaac
and Jacob, and each one
We made a prophet.
50 And We granted them of Our
mercy, and We set for them ˹among
the generations˺ an exalted reverence
˹for all time˺.

51 And mention in the Book
Moses. Indeed, he was chosen,
and he was a messenger, a prophet.
52 And We summoned him from the
right side of Mount al-Ṭûr,
and We brought him near
for close converse.

53 And We granted him, of Our
mercy, his brother Aaron
as a prophet.

54 And mention in the Book
Ishmael. Indeed, he was ever true to
his promise, and he was a messenger,
a prophet.
55 He used to enjoin his family with
the Prayer and Zakât-Charity—and
he was to his Lord ever-pleasing.

56 And mention in the Book
Idrîs. Indeed, he was
ever-truthful, a prophet.
57 And We raised him to a high place.

58 These are the ones upon whom God
bestowed grace—from the prophets
of the children of Adam,
and from those whom We carried
with Noah, and from the children of
Abraham and Israel and from those
whom We guided and selected.
When the verses of the All-Merciful
were recited to them,
they fell to the ground,
bowing down and weeping.

59 Then descending from them
thereafter came descendants who
forsook the Prayer and followed

⌜their⌝ whims, and thus shall they
meet with degradation—
60 except those who repent and believe
and do righteous deeds.
They shall enter the Garden, and
they shall not be wronged in
anything—
61 Gardens of Eden,
which the All-Merciful
has promised His servants in the
unseen. Indeed, it is He whose
promise ever comes true.
62 They shall not hear therein idle talk,
but only, "Peace." And for them
therein shall be their provision,
morning and evening.
63 This is the Garden which We shall
bequeath to those of Our servants
who are God-fearing.

64 ⌜Angel Gabriel says,⌝ "And we, ⌜the
angels,⌝ do not descend,
⌜O Muḥammad,⌝ but at the
command of your Lord.
To Him belongs what is before us
and what is behind us
and what is between this.
And never is your Lord forgetful,
65 Lord of the heavens and the earth
and what is between them;
so worship Him—
and have patience in His worship.

Do you know any other
who ˹bears˺ any semblance to Him?"
66 Man says, "Can it be that when I
have died, I shall ˹again˺
be brought forth alive!"
67 Does man not remember
that We indeed created him before,
and he was nothing?
68 Then, by your Lord,
We shall most surely round them
up, as well as the satans.
Then most surely We shall bring
them around Hell,
on ˹their˺ knees.
69 Then We shall pluck from every
cluster whichever of them
was most intense
in defying the All-Merciful.
70 For We, indeed, are most knowing
about those who are most deserving
of roasting in it.
71 And there is not one of you
but that will come to it.
It is, with your Lord,
an inevitability decreed.
72 Then We shall deliver those
who have been God-fearing;
and We shall leave
the wrongdoers in it,
on ˹their˺ knees.
73 When Our clear verses are recited to
them, those who disbelieve say to
those who believe, "Which of the

two groups, ˹ours or yours,˺
is of a better station
and fairer company?"
74 And how many a generation before
them have We destroyed,
who were of fairer furnishing
and appearance?
75 Say, "Whichever ˹of us˺ is in the
stray way, may the All-Merciful
extend the duration for them—
until ˹the time˺ when suddenly they
see what they have been promised—
whether the torment or the Hour—
then they shall know
who is lowest in position
and weakest in force."
76 Yet God increases those who are
guided with guidance.
And abiding deeds of righteousness
are better with your Lord in reward
and better in return.

77 Then have you seen him who
disbelieved in Our signs and said,
"I shall surely be given wealth
and children"?
78 Has he looked into the Unseen or
has he taken with the All-Merciful
a covenant?
79 No, indeed! We shall surely write
down what he says. And We shall
extend for him the duration
of the torment.

80 And We shall inherit from him what
he speaks of. And he shall
come to Us alone.

81 And they have taken ˹false˺ gods
apart from God, that they may be
for them a ˹means to˺ power.
82 No, indeed! These ˹false gods˺ shall
deny their worship ˹of them˺, and
they shall be as opponents to one
another ˹on the Day of Judgment˺.
83 Have you not seen that We have
sent the satans against
the disbelievers to instigate them
with a vehement instigation?
84 So make no haste concerning them.
We but number for them a
determined number
˹of days and deeds˺
85 ˹until˺ the Day We assemble the
God-fearing before the All-Merciful
in honored delegations,
86 and We shall drive the trespassers
to Hell in droves.
87 None holds the ˹right of˺
intercession except those who have
taken with the All-Merciful
a covenant.

88 And they have said,
"The All-Merciful has taken a son."
89 Truly you have come forth with
something abominable.

90 From it the heavens nearly burst,
and the earth ˹nearly˺ splits and the
mountains ˹nearly˺ fall down,
collapsing,
91 that ˹people˺ should ascribe
to the All-Merciful a son,
92 while it is not befitting to
the All-Merciful that He take a son.
93 Indeed, every being in the heavens
and the earth but comes
to the All-Merciful as a servant.
94 Truly, He has enumerated them,
and He has numbered them
with a precise number.
95 And each one of them
is coming to Him on the Day of
Resurrection alone.
96 As for those who believe and do
righteous deeds, for them the All-
Merciful ordains pure love.

97 Thus We have indeed made ˹this
Quran˺ easy in your tongue, ˹O
Muḥammad,˺ for you to give glad
tidings with it to the God-fearing
and to warn therewith
a contentious people.
98 And how many a generation
have We destroyed before them.
Do you perceive
even one of them
or hear from them
a single sound?

APPENDIX

By Linda Thayer

"Daughter of 'Imrân" and "Sister of Aaron"

The Arabic name *ʿImrân* appears to be equivalent to the anglicized *Amram* of the Bible. The questions that have arisen in connection with this name are twofold: First, Muslim commentators on the Quran have disagreed about the identity of the ʿImrân that the Quran cites in connection with Mary. Second, some non-Muslim commentators on the Quran have speculated about the possible misidentification of Mary with the biblical Miriam. Let us examine the biblical relationships first.

In the Bible, the name *Amram* is given to a man descended from the priestly family line, or "house," of Levi and married to a "daughter of Levi" (Bible, Exodus 2:1). This couple is identified as the parents of Moses, whose earliest days were most precarious (Exodus 2:1–10). The genealogy of Moses

---

Linda Thayer holds her doctoral degree in linguistics. In 1974–79, she served as a Bible Translations Consultant and Linguistics Advisor in West Africa. Her Middle East experience began in 1982–84 when she taught in Bahrain as a Fulbright Exchange Scholar, leading to her acceptance of Islam in time for Ramadan, 1994.

and of his brother Aaron, as sons of *Amram* and *Jochebed* (Exodus 6:20), is recorded as being fully Levitical (Exodus 6:16–20). The special responsibilities and privileges accorded to the genealogical tribe referred to as "the children of Levi" are mentioned throughout the story of the Hebrew people, or "Children of Israel," as recorded in the first several books of the Hebrew, that is, Jewish, Bible. (See Exodus 32:26; Leviticus 6:14–16, 7:6, 8:31; Numbers 1:47–50, 3:5–10, 35:1–3; and Deuteronomy 12:1, 20:14–27.)

It is clear that Moses and Aaron are to be understood as literal progeny of Amram, the son of Kohath, the son of Levi, the son of Jacob ("Israel"), the son of Isaac, the son of Abraham (Exodus 1:1–2, 6:16–20). The Levitical bloodline through their mother is also unmistakable, as Jochebed is identified as a sister of Amram's father (Exodus 6:20).

Now we come to the Biblical "Miriam the prophetess," who is referred to as "the sister of Aaron" (Exodus 15:20–21). Why not "sister of Moses"? Why not "sister of Moses and Aaron"? Whether Miriam was the progeny of the Levitical individuals Amram and Jochebed, or whether her parents were other descendants of the tribe of Levi, we cannot be sure without further evidence, as the older female sibling of Moses is unnamed (Exodus 2:4). While Miriam figures importantly alongside Moses and Aaron (Numbers 12:1-15, 20:1; Micah 6:4), she and Aaron are forced to acknowledge positions subordinate to the biblically described meek-mannered Moses. If Miriam is not a sibling to Moses and Aaron, she at the least bears the honor of a Levitical role (i.e. "sister of Aaron").

When we come to the story of Zachariah and John in the Christian Bible, we find that the parents of the prophet John ("the Baptist") were said both to be descendants of the

Levitical, priestly lines (Luke 1:5–6), as "a certain priest named Zachariah, of the course of Abia [in the wording of the King James Version (KJV)], and his wife was of the daughters of Aaron, and her name was Elizabeth."

The story of Mary and Jesus in the Christian Bible includes a genealogy for Jesus, "the son of David, the son of Abraham" (Matthew 1:1 and Luke 3:21), whose descent is given as being through Jacob's (priestly) son Levi. The Jewish expectation of a Messiah, however, had been tied to the royal line of David and to a prediction regarding Judah (Genesis 49:10). Now the two birth narratives of the Christian New Testament clearly claim that Mary's betrothed husband Joseph was not the biological father of Jesus (Matthew 1:18–20 and Luke 1:24–35, 2:4–5, 2:33), and yet it is Joseph's lineage that is in the Bible as Jesus' Messianic line of descent, or his ancestry!

Surprisingly, it is the Quran, not the Bible, that records Mary's lineage as being through the House of 'Imrân (Quran, 3:33–36 and 66:12). If we accept the biblical genealogies (and if we accept that the Quranic ᶜImrân is the biblical Amram, father of Moses and Aaron), this means that Mary's descent was from Abraham, Isaac, Jacob, Jacob's son Levi, Levi's son Kohath, Kohath's son Amram, Amram's son Aaron. To refer to Mary as *daughter of ᶜImrân* (Quran, 66:12) and as *sister of Aaron* (Quran, 19:28) is not, then, to misidentify the Miriam of the Old Testament Bible with Maryam (Mary), the mother of Jesus in the Quran. These two Quranic titles may rather be seen as identifying the immaculate virgin with the prestigious Levitical family of her Hebrew people, just as John has been identified (in the Bible and, by implication, also in the Quran) with a Levitical parentage.

In addition, the common Quranic identification of Jesus as

son of Mary (Quran, 2:67 and elsewhere) supports the stance of the Eastern Christians who rejected the title "Mother of God" then in use by (Roman) Western Christians. It also implies the parental authority and responsibility entrusted to the devout young Jewish girl, Mary, for properly bringing up God's chosen Messiah. The Jewish people, however, had been referring to the foretold Messiah as "the Son of David" because they had been expecting a kingly ruler to overthrow the power of Rome in Palestine. The Quran's reference to Jesus as "the son of Mary," then, implies concurrence with those Eastern Christians who rejected the philosophical notion of Jesus as "begotten" of God (Bible, John 3:16) and the notion of having a divine essence and agency (John 1:1-14), "the Son of God," "the Word."

The English reader must bear in mind, as well, that in Semitic languages (in both the Hebrew of the Old Testament Bible and the Arabic of the Quran), terms of family relationship—such as father, mother, son, and daughter—were commonly in figurative use. That is, the expressions "son of" or "daughter of," for example, could indicate a descendant or anyone possessing the "characteristics of." While "father of" or "mother of" could mean an ancestor, a prototypical hero, or simply the best example or source of. The expression "children of Adam" (meaning all human beings) or the "Children of Israel" (the Jewish people) can refer to persons hundreds or even thousands of generations removed from Adam or from Israel (that is, Jacob). When Jewish or Christian writers have assumed that the Quran was historically derived from a misunderstanding of biblical texts, they have failed to go beyond the literal words, usually words as found in English translations, either of the Quran or of the biblical texts.

Muslim commentators on the Quran have adopted two basic alternative positions regarding the ᶜImrân that the Quran names in connection with Mary, specifically in terms of the epithets *daughter of ᶜImrân* (that is, Mary herself) and *wife of ᶜImrân* (Mary's mother). One position is consistent with what has been cited here above; namely, that these references identify Mary and her mother with the House of ᶜImrân, ᶜImrân here being the father of Moses and Aaron identified with the priestly Levitical line of the Children of Israel. In this argument, the additional identification of Mary in the Quran as *sister of Aaron* (Quran, 19:28) is a figurative association with Aaron, the prophet and brother of Moses, claiming Aaron's descendants as Mary's lineage.

The second position is that Mary's biological father, and thus her mother's husband, was indeed the ᶜImrân whom God raised to the highest honor, and for whom the third sura of the Quran, called Âl ᶜImrân (the "Family of ᶜImrân") is named. It is he, then, whom the Quran refers to in the verse, *God has surely chosen Adam and Noah, and the Family of Abraham, and the Family of ᶜImrân above all people in the world—descendants, one of another. And God is all-hearing, all-knowing* (Quran, 3:33–34). According to this interpretation, then, ᶜImrân, Mary's father, would have been a true man of God and a patriarch among the Children of Israel in his time. If biblical name histories are to be accepted, and if the father of Moses and Aaron bore the same name as Mary's father, this shows only that the name ᶜImrân, or Amram, was honored among the Children of Israel. And like other people—especially in the ancient world—they named their children after their illustrious forefathers and patriarchs, for which a report of the Prophet ﷺ indicating such a practice has previously been cited.[1] This second position is further strengthened by a look at the Quran's use of the word *imra'ah,* as in "wife" or "wife of," which in none of its instances has been used figuratively, but always literally.

On the issue of lineage, Quran commentators differ. Some relate Mary's heritage to Aaron, the prophet. Others trace the lineage of her father, ʿImrân, to the prophets Solomon and David. It is not clear whether this means that Mary's parents descended from different family lines, the father being from that of David, the mother from that of Aaron. Also relevant is the Quranic epithet *sister of Aaron* (Quran, 19:28), uttered to Mary by her people in shock and dismay when she returned to them with the newborn Jesus عليه السلام. This might imply one of several meanings, one literal and two figurative. It was perhaps a reminder that she came from the noble line of the brother of Moses عليه السلام, the prophet Aaron عليه السلام. It may be a direct reference to a righteous sibling of hers named Aaron. Or it could have been intended as a misguided insult toward her, associating her in a figurative manner with a disreputable man in her community named Aaron. Despite the differing opinions among Quranic scholars, what is crystal clear is that Mary's lineage is certainly from "ʿImrân," whose family possesses one of the two most illustrious genealogies of all time.

APPENDIX NOTES

1. See the notes to the introductory chapter "Mary in the Quran," pp. 11–12.

BIBLIOGRAPHY

ʿAbd al-Raḥmân, ʿÂ'isha [Bint al-Shâṭi', pseud.]. *Al-Tafsîr al-Bayânî li al-Qur'ân al-Karîm*. 2 vols. Cairo: Dâr al-Maʿârif, n.d.

Abû Ḥayyân, Abû ʿAbdullâh Muḥammad ibn Yûsuf ibn ʿAlî al-Andalûsî. *Al-Tafsîr al-Kabîr al-Musammâ bi al-Baḥr al-Muḥîṭ*. 8 vols. Riyâḍ: Maktabat wa Maṭâbiʿ al-Naṣr al-Ḥadîtha, n.d.

Abû al-Saʿûd, Muḥammad ibn Muḥammad al-ʿImâdî. *Tafsîr Abî al-Saʿûd* [or *Irshâd al-ʿAql al-Salîm ilâ Mazâyâ al-Qur'ân al-Karîm*]. 9 vols. in 5. Beirut: Dâr Iḥyâ' al-Turâth al-ʿArabî, n.d.

al-Alûsî, Shihâbuddîn al-Sayyid Maḥmûd. *Rûḥ al-Maʿânî fî Tafsîr al-Qur'ân al-Aẓîm wa Sabʿ al-Mathânî*. 30 vols. in 15. Beirut: Dâr Iḥyâ' al-Turâth al-ʿArabî, n.d.

al-Ashqar, Muḥammad Sulaymân ʿAbdullâh. *Zubdat al-Tafsîr min Fatḥ al-Qadîr*. Kuwait: Wazârat al-Awqâf, 1406/1985.

al-Bayḍâwî, Nâṣiruddîn ʿAbdullâh ibn ʿUmar. *Anwâr al-Tanzîl wa Asrâr al-Ta'wîl* (or *Tafsîr al-Bayḍâwî*). 5 vols. in 2. Beirut: Mu'assasat Shaʿbân, n.d.

al-Bilâdî, ʿÂtiq ibn Ghayth. *Faḍâ'il al-Qur'ân*. Edited by Fârûq Ḥamâda. Makkah: Dâr Makkah, 1410/1990.

Bukhârî, Abû ʿAbdullah Muḥammad Ismâʿîl. *Al-Jâmiʿ al-Ṣaḥîḥ*. 4th edition. 6 vols. Edited by Muṣṭafâ Dîb al-Bughâ. Damascus: Dar Ibn Kathîr, 1990.

al-Dârimî, Abû Muḥammad ʿAbdullah ibn ʿAbd al-Raḥmân. *Sunan Dârimî*. Cairo: Dâr al-Fikr, 1978.

Ehrman, Bart D. *The Orthodox Corruption of Scripture: The Effect of Early Christological Controversies on the Text of the New Testament*. Oxford: Oxford University Press, 1993.

al-Faryâbî, Abû Bakr Jaʿfar ibn Muḥammad ibn al-Ḥasan. *Kitâb Faḍâ'il al-Qur'ân wa Mâ Jâ'a fîhi min al-Faḍl wa fî Kam Yuqra' wa al-Sunna fî Dhâlik*. Edited by Yûsuf ʿUthmân Faḍl Allâh Jibrîl. Riyâḍ: Maktabat al-Rushd, 1989.

Hammad, Ahmad Zaki. *Father of the Flame*. Oak Lawn, Illinois: Quranic Literacy Institute, 1997.

Ibn al-ʿArabî, Abû Bakr Muḥammad ibn ʿAbdullâh. *Aḥkâm al-Qur'ân*. Edited by ʿAlî Muḥammad al-Bijâwî. 2 vols. Beirut: Dâr al-Fikr, n.d.

______. *Qânûn al-Ta'wîl*. Edited by Muḥammad al-Sulaymânî. Beirut: Mu'assasat ʿUlûm al-Qur'ân, 1406/1986.

Ibn ʿÂshûr, Muḥammad al-Ṭâhir. *Tafsîr al-Taḥrîr wa al-Tanwîr*. 15 vols. Cairo: Maktabat Ibn Taymiyya, 1984.

Ibn Ḥajar al-ʿAsqalânî, Aḥmad. *Fatḥ al-Bârî bi Sharḥ Ṣaḥîḥ al-Bukhârî*. 13 vols. Riyâḍ: Maktabat al-Riyâḍ al-Ḥadîtha, n.d.

Ibn Hishâm, Abû Muḥammad ʿAbd al-Malik. *Al-Sîra al-Nabawiyya li Ibn Hishâm*. 4 vols. Edited by Ṭahâ ʿAbd al-Ra'ûf Saʿd. Beirut: Dâr al-Jayd, 1975.

______. *Al-Sîra al-Nabawiyya li Ibn Hishâm*. 4 vols. Edited by Muṣṭafâ al-Saqâ, Ibrâhîm al-Ibyârî, and ʿAbd al-Ḥafîẓ Shalabî. Beirut: Dâr al-Qalam, n.d.

Ibn Kathîr, Imâduddîn Abû al-Fidâ' Ismâ'îl. *Al-Mukhtaṣar Tafsîr Ibn Kathîr.* Edited by Muḥammad 'Alî al-Ṣâbûnî. 3 vols. Beirut: Dâr al-Qur'ân al-Karîm, n.d.

______. *Tafsîr al-Qur'ân al-'Aẓîm.* 4 vols. Beirut: Dâr al-Fikr, n.d.

Ibn Khaldûn, 'Abd al-Raḥmân ibn Muḥammad. *Al-Muqaddima.* 3 vols. Translated by Franz Rosenthal. Princeton, New Jersey: Princeton University Press, 1958.

Ibn Khaldûn, 'Abd al-Raḥmân ibn Muḥammad. *Al-Muqaddimat Ibn Khaldûn.* Beirut: Dâr al-Fikr, n.d.

Ibn al-Qayyim, Shams al-Dîn Muḥammad ibn Abû Bakr ibn Ayyûb ibn Sa'ad ibn Ḥarîz al-Zura'î ibn Qayyim al-Jawziyya. *Al-Tafsîr al-Qayyim li al-Imâm Ibn al-Qayyim.* Compiled by Muḥammad Uways al-Nadwî. Edited by Muḥammad Ḥâmid al-Fiqî. Beirut: Dâr al-Fikr, 1408/1988.

Ibn Taymiyya, Aḥmad ibn 'Abd al-Ḥalîm. *Daqâ'iq al-Tafsîr.* Edited by Muḥammad al-Sayyid. 3d ed. 6 vols. in 3. Beirut: Mu'assasat 'Ulûm al-Qur'ân, 1406/1986.

Ibn 'Uyayna, Sufyân. *Tafsîr Sufyân Ibn 'Uyayna.* Compiled and edited by Aḥmad Ṣâliḥ Maḥâyrî. Beirut: Maktab al-Islâmî; Riyâḍ: Maktabat Usâma, 1403/1983.

'Ilaywî, Ibn Khalîfa. *Jâmi' al-Nuqûl fî Asbâb al-Nuzûl wa Sharḥ Âyâtihâ.* 2 vols. Riyâḍ: Maṭâbi' al-Shu'â', 1404/1984.

'Inâyat, Ghâzî. *Asbâb al-Nuzûl al-Qur'ânî.* Beirut: Dâr al-Jîl, 1991.

al-Mahallî, Jalâluddîn. *Tafsîr al-Imâmayn al-Jalâlayn* (from Sûrat al-Kahf to Sûrat al-Nâs by Jalâluddîn al-Mahallî. From Sûrat al-Baqara to Sûrat al-Isrâ' by al-Suyûṭî). Beirut: Dâr al-Fikr, n.d.

al-Mâwardî, Abû al-Ḥasan 'Alî ibn Ḥabîb. *Tafsîr al-Mâwardî.* 4 vols. Kuwait: Maqhawî Press, 1402/1982.

al-Nasâ'î, Abû 'Abd al-Raḥmân Aḥmad ibn Shu'ayb ibn 'Alî.

Faḍâ'il al-Qur'ân. Edited by Fârûq Ḥamâda. Beirut: Dâr Iḥyâ' al-ʿUlûm; al-Dâr al-Bayḍâ' [Casablanca]: Dâr al-Thaqâfa, 1413/1992.

Polkinghorne, John. *Beyond Science: A Wider Context*. Cambridge: Cambridge University Press, 1998.

al-Qâsimî, Muḥammad Jamâluddin. *Tafsîr al-Qur'ân*. 17 vols. in 10. Beirut: Dâr al-Fikr, 1978.

al-Qurṭubî, Abû ʿAbdullâh Muḥammad ibn Aḥmad al-Anṣârî. *Al-Jâmiʿ li Aḥkâm al-Qur'ân*. 20 vols. Cairo: Dâr al-Kutub al-Miṣriyya, 1952–67.

Quṭb, Muḥammad. *Dirâsât Qur'âniyya*. 3d ed. Beirut (and Cairo): Dâr al-Shurûq, 1402/1982.

Quṭb, Sayyid. *Fî Ẓilâl al-Qur'ân*. 6 vols. Beirut: Dâr al-Shurûq, 1393/1973.

al-Râzî, al-Fakhr. *Al-Tafsîr al-Kabîr*. 3d ed. 32 vols. in 15. Beirut: Dâr Iḥyâ' al-Turâth al-ʿArabî, n.d.

Riḍâ, Muḥammad Rashîd. *Tafsîr al-Qur'an al-Ḥakîm* (known as *Tafsîr al-Manâr*). 2d ed. 12 vols. Beirut: Dâr al-Maʿrifa, n.d.

al-Ṣâbûnî, Muḥammad ʿAlî, ed. *Ṣafwat al-Tafâsîr*. 4th ed. 3 vols. Beirut: Dâr al-Qur'ân al-Karîm, 1402/1981.

Shaltût, Maḥmûd. *Tafsîr al-Qur'ân al-Karîm*. 6th ed. Beirut: Dâr al-Shurûq, 1394/1974.

al-Shawkânî, Muḥammad ibn ʿAlî ibn Muḥammad. *Fatḥ al-Qadîr*. 5 vols. Beirut: Dâr Iḥyâ' al-Turâth al-ʿArabî, n.d.

______. *Nayl al-Awṭâr*. 9 vols. Beirut: Dâr al-Jîl, 1973.

al-Suddî al-Kabîr, Abû Muḥammad Ismâʿîl ibn ʿAbd al-Raḥmân. *Tafsîr al-Suddî al-Kabîr*. Compiled by Muḥammad ʿAṭâ Yûsuf. Manṣûra: Dâr al-Wafâ', 1993.

al-Suyûṭî, ʿAbd al-Raḥmân ibn al-Kamâl Jamâluddin. *Al-Itqân fî ʿUlûm al-Qur'ân*. Edited by Muḥammad Abû al-Faḍl Ibrâhîm. 3d ed. Cairo: Dâr al-Turâth, 1985.

______. *Lubâb al-Nuqûl fî Asbâb al-Nuzûl*. Beirut: Dâr Iḥyâ' al-ʿUlûm, 1978.

______. *Tafsîr al-Durr al-Manthûr fî al-Tafsîr al-Ma'thûr*. 8 vols. Beirut: Dâr al-Fikr, 1403/1983.

______. *Tafsîr al-Imâmayn al-Jalâlayn* (from Sûrat al-Kahf to Sûrat al-Nâs by Jalâluddîn al-Maḥallî. From Sûrat al-Baqara to Sûrat al-Isrâ' by al-Suyûṭî). Beirut: Dâr al-Fikr, n.d.

al-Ṭabarî, Abû Jaʿfar Muḥammad ibn Jarîr. *Jâmiʿ al-Bayân ʿan Ta'wîl [ây] al-Qur'ân*. 3d ed. 30 vols. in 12. Cairo: Al-Ḥalabî Press, 1968.

______. *Jâmiʿ al-Bayân fî Tafsîr al-Qur'ân*. 12 vols. Beirut: Dâr al-Kutub al-ʿIlmiyya, 1412/1992.

______. *Mukhtaṣar Tafsîr al-Ṭabarî*. Edited by Muḥammad ʿAlî al-Ṣâbûnî and Ṣâliḥ Aḥmad Riḍâ. 2 vols. Beirut: Dâr al-Qur'ân al-Karîm, 1403/1983.

al-Thawrî, ibn ʿAbdullâh Sufyân ibn Saʿîd. *Tafsîr Sufyân al-Thawrî*. Beirut: Dâr al-Kutb al-ʿIlmiyya, 1403/1983.

U. A. E. Ministry. *Al-Muntakhab fî Tafsîr al-Qur'ân al-Karîm*. United Arab Emirates: U. A. E. Ministry, n.d.

al-Wâdiʿî, Abû ʿAbd al-Raḥmân Muqbil ibn Hâdî. *Al-Ṣaḥîḥ al-Musnad min Asbâb al-Nuzûl*. 4th ed. Cairo: Maktabat Ibn Taymiyya, 1408/1987.

al-Wâḥidî, Abî al-Ḥasan ʿAlî Aḥmad. *Asbâb al-Nuzûl*. Edited by Ayman Ṣâliḥ Shaʿbân. Cairo: Dâr al-Ḥadîth, n.d.

______. *Al-Wasîṭ fî Tafsîr al-Qur'ân al-Majîd*. 4 vols. Beirut: Dâr al-Fikr al-ʿIlmiyya, 1994.

Yâqût, Shihâb al-Dîn Abû Abdullah. *Muʿjam al-Buldân*. 5 vols. Beirut: Dâr Ṣâdir, 1977.

al-Ẓâhirî, Abû Turâb. *Shawâhid al-Qur'ân*. 2 vols. Jeddah: Literary Cultural Club, 1989.

al-Zamakhsharî, Maḥmûd ibn ʿUmar ibn Muḥammad. *Al-Kashshâf ʿan Ḥaqâ'iq al-Tanzîl wa ʿUyûn al-Aqâwîl fî Wujûh al-Ta'wîl*. 4 vols. Beirut: Dâr al-Maʿrifa, n.d.

al-Zarkashî, Badruddîn. *Al-Burhân fî ʿUlûm al-Qur'ân*. 3d ed. Edited by Muḥammad Abû Faḍl Ibrâhîm. 4 vols. n.p.: Dâr al-Fikr, 1980.

Zaylaʿî, Jamâluddîn Abû Muḥammad ʿAbdullâh ibn Yûsuf al-Ḥanafî. *Nasb al-Râyyah li Aḥâdîth al-Hidâya*. 2d ed. 4 vols. n.p.: Al-Maktaba al-Islâmiyya, 1973.

al-Zuḥaylî, Wahba. *Al-Tafsîr al-Munîr fî al-ʿAqîda wa al-Sharîʿa wa al-Manhaj*. 32 parts in 16 vols. Beirut: Dâr al-Fikr al-Muʿâṣir; Damascus: Dâr al-Fikr, 1411/1991.

SUBJECT INDEX

SPECIAL INDEX

AN INDEX OF JESUS, JOHN, MARY, AND ZACHARIAH IN THE ENTIRE QURAN. THE CONTEXT IS FOLLOWED BY THE QURAN'S SURA AND VERSE NUMBERS.

(INDEX PREPARED BY IBRAHIM ABUSHARIF)

JESUS (ʿÎsâ) عليه السلام

JOHN (Yaḥyâ ﷺ)

Among the prefered of the world: 6:86–87

Commanded to take the Book with power: 19:12

Confirming a word from God: 3:39

Given wisdom, compassion, and purity: 19:12–13

Glading tidings of, to father Zacharia: 3:39–41, 19:7–9

Godfearingness of: 19:13

Granted to Zacharia: 21:90

Guided by God: 6:85

Honorable prophet: 3:39

"Peace be upon him": 19:15

Righteousness of: 3:39, 6:85

Unique name of: 19:7

Virtuous to parents: 19:14

MARY (Maryam)

Peace be upon her

Accepted by God with good acceptance: 3:37

Angels' visitation with tidings of a son: 3:45–47, 19:17–21

Children of Israel speaking ill of Mary: 4:156

Chosen above the women of the world: 3:42

Conceiving Jesus and giving birth: 19:22–26

Confirming the word of God: 66:12

Daughter of ʿImrân, 66:12

Family of, outraged over her having a son: 19:27–29

Given provision by God in the Sanctuary: 3:37

Given shelter on a hilltop: 23:50

God's grace upon: 5:110

God's spirit breathed into her: 21:91, 66:12

Jesus' mother, as in "son of Mary" (a common reference): 2:87, 2:253, 3:45, 4:157, 4:171, 5:17, 5:46, 5:72, 5:75, 5:78, 5:109, 5:112, 5:114, 5:116, 9:31, 19:34, 23:50, 33:7, 43:57, 57:27, 61:6, 61:14

Jesus virtuous to: 19:32

Mother of, dedicating her to God: 3:35–36

Named by her mother: 3:36

Not a diety: 5:116

People contending over the care of: 3:44

Preserving her chastity: 21:91, 66:12

Reverential to God: 3:43, 66:12

Sign to humanity: 21:91, 23:50

ZACHARIA (Zakariyya ﷺ)

ALSO BY THE AUTHOR

LASTING PRAYERS

of the Quran and the Prophet Muḥammad ﷺ

THE MOST COMPREHENSIVE volume of supplications from the Quran and the Prophet Muḥammad ﷺ in the English language, *Lasting Prayers* presents a lucid, bold, and moving account of the Quran's "heroes of prayer" and compiles the supplications of the Prophet ﷺ that cover the full sweep of life's occasions. As reviewer Dr. Linda Thayer writes:

> *Lasting Prayers* discloses the height and depth, the length and breadth of Islamic spiritual energy. The all-inclusive introduction summons the hesitant to come close to God, to come boldly before his Lord, who stands ever ready to give and to forgive generously. By allowing oneself to become absorbed into the prayers recorded in the Quran and those spoken from the lips of the Prophet Muḥammad ﷺ himself, the seeker establishes a dynamic relationship with the Creator. In summary, the compilation of prayers in this comprehensive book serves to teach the *"muslim"* to be ever sensitive to his intended purpose on earth, to his own standing before God, to his social interaction, and to the entire creation's incessant need for and welcome access to Allah. One learns how to ask God's blessing for this life and for the Next.

And as Dr. Ahmad Sakr writes:

> The writing style of the book is profound—highly literary in approach but easy to read and understand. I do recommend this book to all readers of English: the politician and the lawyer; the social service worker, the physician, the nurse, and the sick; the professor, the student, the librarian. Such individuals and many more do need this book to use in their daily lives.

بسم الله الرحمن الرحيم

AI-AZHAR AL-SHARIF
ISLAMIC RESEARCH ACADEMY
GENERAL DEPARTMENT
For Research, Writing & Translation

الازهر الشريف
مجمع البحوث الإسلامية
الإدارة العامة
للبحوث والتاليف والترجمة

Dr. Ahmad Zaki Hammad

Book Review

Lasting Prayers of the Quran and the Prophet Muḥammad ﷺ

With reference to your letter dated 19 August 1996, in respect of your request that this department review your book: **Lasting Prayers of the Quran and the Prophet Muhammad ﷺ** :

We convey to you that this book comprises beneficial knowledge concerning the prayers of the Quran and the Prophet Muhammad ﷺ.

Having reviewed the book as requested, we have the pleasure to declare that we have no objection that this book be put in circulation or introduced for republication.

Thank you.

General Director

١٩٩٦/١١/٢١

THE OPENING TO THE QURAN

Commentary & Vocabulary Reference of al-Fâtiḥa

"The Opening" chapter (or sura) of the Quran—called al-Fâtiḥa—is undoubtedly the most often recited portion of revealed scripture in the world. Its impact on the psyche and soul of more than a fifth of the human family cannot be overstated. One who comes close to the meaning and import of its seven sacred verses draws near indeed to understanding the religion of Islam and the Muslim men and women who seek to follow its "straight way." In *The Opening to the Quran,* a leading scholar of the Quran (the Muslim scripture), Dr. Ahmad Zaki Hammad, guides the English-speaking reader through the gateway of the Quran and to the treasure trove of vivid meanings and penetrating themes of this concise sura and the ever universal Book it opens.

"The format, substance, and writing are superb."

— *Dr. Robert Crane, Editorial Consultant, Washington, D.C.*

"I am deeply inspired by this new interpretation. The English reads well and is accurately close to its original Arabic. The Commentary is very prayerful. It helps the reader to come closer to the Word of God and enjoy its riches."

— *Dr. Muzzammil Siddiqi, Director, Islamic Center, Orange County, CA*

"The interpretation is clear and smooth. The Overview and Commentary . . . extract such deep religious experience. I think [the] discourse is most edifying."

— *Dr. Willis Gertner, Prof. of Religious Studies, Univ. of Wisconsin*

بسم الله الرحمن الرحيم

AI-AZHAR AL-SHARIF
ISLAMIC RESEARCH ACADEMY
GENERAL DEPARTMENT
For Research, Writing & Translation

الازهر الشريف
مجمع البحوث الإسلامية
الإدارة العامة
للبحوث والتاليف والترجمة

Dr. Ahmad Zaki Hammad

Book Review
The Opening to the Quran

With reference to your letter dated 19 August 1996, in respect of your request that this department review your book: **The Opening to the Quran: Commentary and Vocabulary Reference of al-Fatiha**:

We convey to you that this book comprises beneficial knowledge concerning the commentary and vocabulary referencc of al-Fatiha.

Having reviewed the book as requested, we have the pleasure to declare that we have no objection that this book be put in circulation or introduced for republication.

Thank you.

General Director

١٩٩٦/١١/٢١

FATHER OF THE FLAME

Commentary & Vocabulary Reference of Sûrat al-Masad

It is most instructive to touch on the motives, strategies, and means of the Qurayshite opposition to Islam in the context of Sûrat al-Masad (111), for it is the only sura of the Quran that mentions by name an antagonist of the Prophet ﷺ, for which the student of the Quran must suspect a much deeper reason than mere condemnation of the sura's villains. Not surprisingly, in the person and personality of Abû Lahab (and of his wife) one finds unfolded certain essential aspects of the larger Makkan opposition exemplified for closer examination. Also, one cannot fail to note that ultimately it is this opposition to the godly way of life that the Quran holds forth as the paradigm of human hostility to faith. As a reviewer writes:

> *Father of the Flame* is a multi-leveled work. The Introduction sets the scene and gives the context of the sura. The Interpretation brings the sura alive. The Vocabulary Reference is a more scholarly treatment of the sura's chief words, which aids the reader to attain independent understanding. All of this makes the book appeal to a wide range of readers. Having been reading a number of recently published books on Muḥammad ﷺ, I am struck by the superiority of this piece of work. The centrality of the Quran in the mission of the Prophet ﷺ—telling the Prophet's story with key references from the Quran—gives true depth and solidity to the story. There is no defensive posture, simply positive addressing of relevant issues.

— E. A. Martin

The following is a statement of endorsement for the publication,

Father of the Flame,

issued by **AL-AZHAR AL-SHARIF**

Islamic Research Academy

General Department For Research Writing & Translation.

Date of issue: 5 Ṣafar 1417 / June 10, 1997.

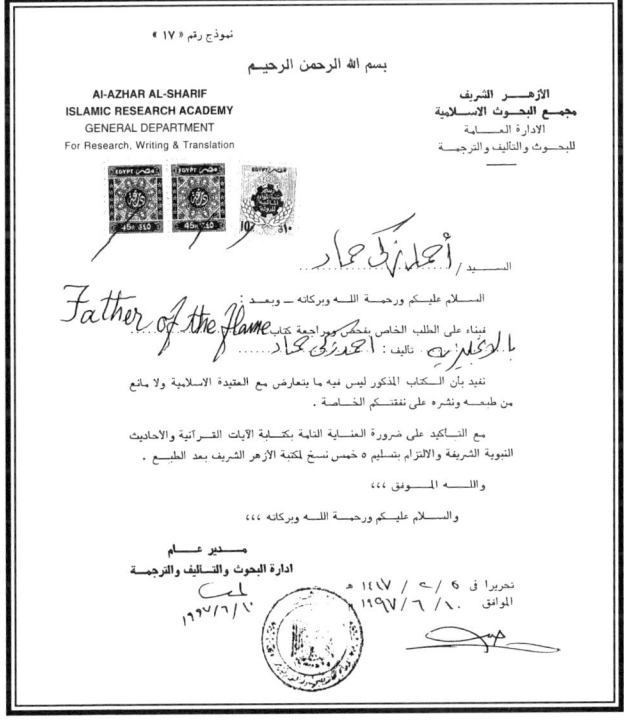

نموذج رقم « ١٧ »

بسم الله الرحمن الرحيم

AI-AZHAR AL-SHARIF **ISLAMIC RESEARCH ACADEMY** GENERAL DEPARTMENT For Research, Writing & Translation	**الأزهـــــر الشريف** **مجمـــع البحـــوث الاســـلامية** الادارة العـــــامة للبحـــوث والتأليف والترجمـــة

السـيد / أحمد زكي حماد

السـلام عليـكم ورحمـة اللـه وبركاته ـ وبعـد :

فبناء على الطلب الخاص بفحص ومراجعة كتاب Father of the Flame بالانجليزية تأليف : أحمد زكي حماد

نفيد بأن الـكتاب المذكور ليس فيه ما يتعارض مع العقيدة الاسلامية ولا مانع من طبعـه ونشره على نفقتـكم الخـاصة .

مع التـأكيد على ضرورة العنـاية التامة بكتـابة الآيات القـرآنية والأحاديث النبوية الشريفة والالتزام بتسليم ٥ خمس نسخ لمكتبة الأزهر الشريف بعد الطبـع .

واللـه المـوفق ،،،

والسـلام عليـكم ورحمـة اللـه وبركاته ،،،

مـدير عـام

ادارة البحوث والتـأليف والترجمـة

١٩٩٧/٦/١٠

تحريرا فى ٥ / ص / ١٤١٧ هـ

الموافق ١٠ / ٦ / ١٩٩٧ م

ONE GOD

Commentary & Vocabulary Reference of Sûrat al-Ikhlâṣ

The verses of the Quran mention attributes and characteristics of God that accord with His worthiness and oneness. They form an unbroken hymn that frees the human soul and illuminates it with a sense of the Divine Being's magnificence and splendor. This is especially true of the four short verses of Sûrat al-Ikhlâṣ. — One God: The Everlasting Refuge

From the very beginning, human beings have sought to know more about God—an impulse that has affected every aspect of human life and culture. The sheer volume of religious literature on this topic is, to say the least, imposing. Yet Islam's own imposing body of literature on God and His attributes remains beyond common access in the English language. The present volume—a vital contribution to Islamic literature—presents the English reader with an authoritative synthesis of one of the Quran's most seminal suras (or chapters), Sûrat al-Ikhlâṣ. *One God* contains an ***Interpretation*** of the sura's message; an ***Overview*** of the background of its revelation; an extensive ***Commentary*** on God's divine nature; a summary, ***Rules and Merits***, that highlights Sûrat al-Ikhlâṣ in Muslim worship; and an extensive discussion in the ***Vocabulary Reference*** on the words that make up this beautiful sura. It is likely that readers will be giving this book to friends, neighbors, and colleagues for generations to come. And seekers of religious truth perhaps will be eager to read its erudite explication of how the final expression of the monotheistic faiths conveys to humanity the heavenly discourse on the one true God.

The following is a statement of endorsement for the publication,

One God: The Everlasting Refuge,

issued by **AL-AZHAR AL-SHARIF**

Islamic Research Academy

General Department For Research Writing & Translation.

Date of issue: 5 Ṣafar 1417 / June 10, 1997.

نموذج رقم « ١٧ »

بسم الله الرحمن الرحيم

الأزهر الشريف
مجمع البحوث الاسلامية
الادارة العامة
للبحوث والتأليف والترجمة

Al-AZHAR AL-SHARIF
ISLAMIC RESEARCH ACADEMY
GENERAL DEPARTMENT
For Research, Writing & Translation

السيد / أحمد زكي حماد

السلام عليكم ورحمة الله وبركاته — وبعد :

فبناء على الطلب الخاص بفحص ومراجعة كتاب : One God بالإنجليزية تأليف : أحمد زكي حماد

نفيد بأن الكتاب المذكور ليس فيه ما يتعارض مع العقيدة الاسلامية ولا مانع من طبعه ونشره على نفقتكم الخاصة .

مع التأكيد على ضرورة العناية التامة بكتابة الآيات القرآنية والأحاديث النبوية الشريفة والالتزام بتسليم ٥ خمس نسخ لمكتبة الأزهر الشريف بعد الطبع .

والله الموفق ،،،

والسلام عليكم ورحمة الله وبركاته ،،،

تحريرا في ٥ / ٢ / ١٤١٧ هـ
الموافق ١٠ / ٦ / ١٩٩٧ م

مدير عام
ادارة البحوث والتأليف والترجمة
١٩٩٧/٦/١٠

ISLAMIC LAW

Understanding Juristic Differences

While interest in Islamic law is on the rise in the English-speaking world, there remains the need for greater accessibility and understanding of its issues and sources. Of all its aspects, however, least has been written on the topic of *al-Khilâf al-Fiqhi*, the science exploring the world of juristic differences. In *Islamic Law: Understanding Juristic Differences*, Dr. Ahmad Zaki Hammad introduces the major principles governing juristic variance among established schools of law and well-known Muslim jurists, and their different methods of interpreting texts from the Quran and the statements and deeds of the Prophet Muḥammad ﷺ. *Islamic Law* outlines the major categories of *khilâf*. It then surveys more than a dozen subcategories, delving into actual readings and interpretations of legal texts from the Quran and statements of the Prophet ﷺ, from the point of view of several schools of Islamic jurisprudence. As Dr. Abd al-Hakim S. Jackson wrote in the preface to the work:

> *Islamic Law* makes a stunning contribution by laying bare the issue of juristic variance, explaining its causes and distinguishing those forms that are legitimate from those that are not. Dr. Hammad guides the reader to a fascinating rediscovery of the spirit of tolerance and mutual recognition in Islam.

QURANIC LITERACY INSTITUTE

Mary: The Chosen Woman is one of a series of publications of THE QURAN: INTERPRETATION IN CONTEXT,™ an endeavor of THE QURAN PROJECT™ and a premier undertaking of the QURANIC LITERACY INSTITUTE (QLI).™ QLI's mission—symbolized by its motto "Advancing Islamic Literacy"™—is to alleviate Islamic illiteracy among the human family and, in the words of the QLI Charter, ***"to aid men, women, and families of all creeds and all walks of life to understand the seminal sources of Islam and to help Muslims live Islam as a way of life."***

QURANIC LITERACY INSTITUTE

P.O. Box 1467 • Bridgeview, Illinois 60455 • U.S.A.
(708) 430-1991 (Tel) • (708) 430-1992 (Fax)

ABOUT THE AUTHOR

The author, Dr. Ahmad Zaki Hammad, is a leading scholar on the Quran and the principal sources of Islam. He is the author of the well-received *Lasting Prayers of the Quran and the Prophet Muḥammad* ﷺ. As part of his work, **THE QURAN: INTERPRETATION IN CONTEXT**, he has written the widely acclaimed books *The Opening to the Quran: Commentary & Vocabulary Reference of al-Fâtiḥa*; *Father of the Flame: Commentary & Vocabulary Reference of Sûrat al-Masad*; *One God: Commentary & Vocabulary Reference of Sûrat al-Ikhlâṣ*; and *The Fairest of Stories: The Life Story of Joseph Son of Jacob in the Quran*. He has also written *Islamic Law: Understanding Juristic Differences* and the study and translation of al-Ghazâlî's quintessential work on Islamic jurisprudence, *al-Mustaṣfâ min ʿIlm al-Uṣûl*. Dr. Hammad received his Islamic and Arabic training at the world's foremost center of Islamic learning, al-Azhar University, Cairo, and was awarded the graduate degree of *ʿĀlamiyya* from the Faculty of Theology. He also holds a Ph.D. in Islamic Studies from the University of Chicago.